GUARDING THE GOLDFIELDS

The Story of the Yukon Field Force

by
Brereton Greenhous

Maps by William R. Constable

Toronto and Oxford
Dundurn Press
1987

in collaboration with
the Canadian War Museum
Canadian Museum of Civilization
National Museums of Canada
(Canadian War Museum Historical Publication No. 24)

Design and Production:Andy Tong
Printing and Binding:Gagné Printing Ltd., Louiseville, Quebec, Canada

The publisher wishes to acknowledge the generous assistance and ongoing support of **The Canada Council, The Book Publishing Industry Development Programme** of the **Department of Communications** and **The Ontario Arts Council.**

Care has been taken to trace the ownership of copyright material used in the text (including the illustrations). The author and publisher welcome any information enabling them to rectify any reference or credit in subsequent editions.

In the writing of this book the inferences drawn and the opinions expressed are those of the author himself, and the National Museums of Canada are in no way responsible for his reading or presentation of the facts as stated.

J. Kirk Howard, Publisher

Cataloguing in Publication

Lester, Edward, 1861 -1938
  Guarding the Goldfields

Includes the diary of Edward Lester.
Bibliography: p.
Includes index.
ISBN 1-55002-028-5

1. Canada. Canadian Army. Yukon Field Force. 2. Klondike River Valley (Yukon) - Gold discoveries. 3. Yukon Territory - History - 1895-1918* 4. Lester, Edward, 1861-1938 - Diaries. 5. Soldiers - Yukon Territory - Diary. I. Greenhous, Brereton, 1929- . II. Title.

FC4022.3.L48 1987   971.9'102   C87-094968-3
F1093.L48 1987

Dundurn Press Limited
1558 Queen Street East
Toronto, Canada
M4L 1E8

Dundurn Distribution Limited
Athol Brose, School Hill,
Wargrave, Reading
England
RG10 8DY

Canadian War Museum Historical Publications

Series editor: Fred Gaffen

Previous Titles in the Series

[1] *Canada and the First World War*, by John Swettenham. Canadian War Museum, Ottawa, 1968. Bilingual. OUT OF PRINT.
[2] *D-Day*, by John Swettenham. Canadian War Museum, Ottawa, 1969. Bilingual. OUT OF PRINT.
[3] *Canada and the First World War*, by John Swettenham. Based on the Fiftieth Anniversary Armistice Display at the Canadian War Museum. Ryerson, Toronto, 1969. Published in paperback. McGraw-Hill Ryerson, 1973. OUT OF PRINT.
[4] *Canadian Military Aircraft*, by J.A. Griffin. Queen's Printer, Ottawa. OUT OF PRINT.
5. *The Last War Drum: The North West Campaign of 1885*, by Desmond Morton. Hakkert, Toronto, 1972.
6. *The Evening of Chivalry*, by John Swettenham. National Museums of Canada, Ottawa, 1972. French edition available.
7. *Valiant Men: Canada's Victoria Cross and George Cross Winners*, ed. by John Swettenham. Hakkert, Toronto, 1973. OUT OF PRINT.
8. *Canada Invaded, 1775-1776*, by George Stanley. Hakkert, Toronto, 1973. French edition available.
9. *The Canadian General, Sir William Otter*, by Desmond Morton. Hakkert, Toronto, 1974. Bilingual.
10. *Silent Witnesses*, by John Swettenham and Herbert F. Wood. Hakkert, Toronto, 1974. French edition available.
11. *Broadcast from the Front: Canadian Radio Overseas in the Second World War*, by A.E. Powley. Hakkert, Toronto, 1975.
12. *Canada's Fighting Ships*, by K.R. Macpherson. Samuel Stevens Hakkert, Toronto, 1975.
13. *Canada's Nursing Sisters*, by G.W. L. Nicholson. Samuel Stevens Hakkert, Toronto, 1975. OUT OF PRINT.
14. *RCAF: Squadron Histories and Aircraft, 1924-1968*, by Samuel Kostenuk and John Griffin. Samuel Stevens Hakkert, Toronto, 1975. OUT OF PRINT.
15. *Canada's Guns: An Illustrated History of Artillery*, by Leslie W.C.S. Barnes. National Museums of Canada, Ottawa, 1979. French edition available.
16. *Military Uniforms in Canada 1665-1970*, by Jack L. Summers and René Chartrand, and illustrated by R.J. Marrion. National Museums of Canada, Ottawa, 1981. French edition available.
17. *Canada at Dieppe*, by T. Murray Hunter. Balmuir, Ottawa, 1982. French edition available.
18. *The War of 1812: Land Operations*, by George F. G. Stanley. Macmillan of Canada. Toronto, 1983. French edition available.
19. *1944: The Canadians in Normandy*, by Reginald H. Roy. Macmillan of Canada, Toronto, 1984, French edition available.
20. *Redcoats and Patriotes: The Rebellions in Lower Canada, 1837-38*, by Elinor Kyte Senior. Canada's Wings, Stittsville, Ontario, 1985. French edition available.
21. *Sam Hughes: The Public Career of a Controversial Canadian*, 1885-1916, by Ronald G. Haycock. Wilfrid Laurier University Press, Waterloo, Ontario, 1986.
22. *General Sir Arthur Currie: A Military Biography*, by A.M. J. Hyatt. University of Toronto Press, Toronto, 1987.
23. *Volunteers and Redcoats — Rebels and Raiders, A Military History of the Rebellions in Upper Canada*, by Mary Beacock Fryer. Dundurn Press, Toronto and Oxford, 1987.

For further information on these titles, please write to the Canadian War Museum, Canadian Museum of Civilization, National Museums of Canada, Ottawa, Canada K1A 0M8

For his sons
this book is dedicated to the memory of

GERALD G. CUMMING
archivist *par excellence*

born 18 September 1944; died 18 July 1986

TABLE OF CONTENTS

PREFACE
Acknowledgements

I n the preparation of this book I have been much helped by my colleague, Dr. W.J. McAndrew, who co-authored an article on the Field Force, published in the *Canadian Defence Quarterly* in the spring of 1981. I also owe a great debt to Major Ken Eyre, CD (Retd), whose doctoral thesis for King's College, London was a convenient and valuable reference work on the political background to the formation of the Field Force. Peter Robertson helped with the photographs and drew my attention to the Woodside-Evans correspondence in the Woodside Papers at the Public Archives of Canada. Stan Horrall and Bill Beahen of the RCMP Historical Section provided brief biographies of the 'Mounties' mentioned in the text.

Colonel Phil Spencer and his staff at Wolsely Barracks searched the Regimental Archives there for biographical material on Lester. M. Marcel Piché of the Department of Veterans' Affairs and Mrs. J.C. McDonald of the Victorian Order of Nurses took time to help me from their busy schedules.

Writing about the long march of the Field Force is one thing; covering the same ground is another, and words cannot express my gratitude to Major G.M. Currie, CD, then the officer commanding B Company, First Battalion of The Royal Canadian Regiment, who agreed to take a middle-aged historian along when he and his men retraced the route of the Field Force in the summer of 1983. There were more than ninety of us on the trail — including nine from the Second Regiment of The Royal Canadian Horse Artillery — and to mention every name is hardly practicable. Some come easily to mind — Master Warrant Officer George MacEachern, after me the oldest man on the trail, the indefatigable Sergeants Willard MacIsaac and Rod Conrad, Sergeant Doug MacLean, a wizard with the machete. A good many of the lads were Maritimers or Newfoundlanders, which was just as well, for we caught and ate a lot of fish! I remember them all with great affection.

Brereton Greenhous
Ottawa, 10 September 1987

INTRODUCTION

"THE GOLDEN MECCA OF THE NORTH"

The work which follows (a blend of conventional research and reconstruction and first-person accounts which I hope provides a more complete and interesting account than either used alone) constitutes a history of the Yukon Field Force, an *ad hoc* unit of the Canadian Militia which only existed for two years, from 1898 until 1900. It was created for two closely-related, and still relevant, reasons. First, to present a symbol of Canadian sovereignty in a remote part of the country — a need which has arisen from time to time in our history and is certainly still with us today — and, secondly, to provide as much aid to the civil power as the authori-

A street scene in Dawson, circa 1898.

7

ties might require to maintain law and order in the turbulent society of the goldfields.

On the surface, the Field Force did little more than reach the goldfields, fight fires, perform a great number of ceremonial and bullion guards, and maintain itself in that hostile environment. But its sojourn in the Yukon marked the first time that Canadian troops had ventured — and wintered — north of 60° despite the fact that a third of this country's land mass lies above that latitude, and it would be half a century before anything similar was done again. Moreover, the effective way in which the Force operated, and the discipline it demonstrated, did something to dispel the long-standing popular images — assiduously furthered by the Volunteer Militia — of the Permanent Force, Canada s regular soldiers, as 'barrack soldiers', fit only for the parade square, or 'snowbirds', joining in the fall and deserting in the spring.

The perceived threat to sovereignty came from Americans. There was never any question of the United States' government plotting annexation, but at least eighty percent of the population

The Dawson waterfront in gold rush days

8

of the Yukon in 1898 were Americans, few of them docile, and virtually every one with a personal firearm of some kind. There were only some two hundred policemen to maintain law and order and, as the correspondent of *The Times* of London reported on the eve of the Force's arrival there:

> It is deplorable to have to admit, but idle to ignore, the fact that the administration of the Klondike district, and the relations which exist between the Government and the public, leave almost everything to be desired... . There is a widely prevalent conviction not only that the laws are bad, but that the officers through whom they are administered are corrupt.[1]

Despite the legend of effortless Mounted Police superiority, the newly-appointed Commissioner for the Yukon Territory, Major J.M. Walsh— a distinguished former 'Mountie' himself — wondered if his Minister appreciated "how thoroughly this district is in the hands of a foreign element" and felt that "it would be the easiest thing in the world for a few bold men to take possession.... If such a thing did happen, not another Canadian Policeman or soldier would be permitted to cross the United States territory to reach this district... ."[2]

Such a locally-planned, pro-American *coup*, brought about by frustration over inappropriate mining regulations and their inept or dishonest application, and then carried through along the general lines of those which had earlier brought both California and Oregon into the American union, may have been unlikely but was always a possibility. However, the proximity of a formed body of well-armed troops, held in ready reserve was bound to discourage precipitate action on the part of malcontents. The Field Force may well have played a greater role in the evolution of Canada than the record would indicate.

There are a number of reasons why historians have paid little attention to the history of the Force, not the least of them being the research effort required to exhume the relevant documentation from the voluminous and poorly-organised files of the Adjutant-General's correspondence. The process bears some resemblance to the turn-of-the-century moiling for gold in the Yukon, for nuggets of information are scattered thinly among multifarious applications from patronage seekers, endless memoranda on administrative trivia, and weekly, monthly, annual returns dealing with everything from ammunition expenditures to janitorial services in militia armouries from Halifax to Victoria.

In the newspapers of the day, which certainly emphasised the stampede to the goldfields and which one might expect to be fruitful sources, reports on the Field Force were usually trimmed in favour of human interest stories on the Klondikers who had struck it rich or had lost everything they owned — or sometimes done both in quick succession. Only when the Force departed from Ottawa, or passed through Winnipeg or Vancouver, and again when "lying letters to the Newspapers"[3] announced a mutiny in the ranks, did the troops get much attention. Their struggle north, over the so-called 'all Canadian' route, the Teslin trail, was an epic in itself, but travel agents had not yet coined the slogan that 'getting there is half the fun'.

In any case, popular attention was fixed on the more spectacular Skagway and Dyea routes that led over the White and Chilcoot passes respectively. Those were the quickest ways into the Yukon, taken by Uncle George and Cousin Bert — and perhaps even Sister Kate — as well as most of the newspaper correspondents. That was where the action was. A classic picture showing a long, black line of stampeders toiling up the snow-clogged Chilcoot Pass in the winter of '97, and the 'Dead Horse Trail' sobriquet applied to the White Pass route, had already caught and held the public eye in a way that the more mundane, but just as demanding, Teslin trail never could.

The international news was just as overwhelming. The departure of the Field Force from Ottawa came in the shadow of Admiral Dewey's attack on a Spanish naval squadron in Manila Bay, the opening blow of the Spanish-American War that dominated the headlines through the summer. By September the British conquest of the Sudan, avenging the murder of General Charles 'Chinese' Gordon thirteen years earlier, had begun, and then, in November, came word of the Fashoda incident that carried France and Great Britain to the brink of war.

All these events tended to drive news of the Field Force on to the back pages when it earned a mention at all, but worse was to come. The following year, when the gold rush had subsided into a leisurely shuffle, the Spanish had accepted defeat, and the British were graciously imposing imperial values on the 'fuzzy-wuzzies', political and economic turmoil in the South African goldfields boiled over into war. By the end of 1899 British pride had been thoroughly humbled and a Canadian contingent was on its way to the South African battlefields. Half of the Field Force had already been withdrawn; before the final withdrawal of the Yukon garrison was announced, a second Canadian contingent was on the high veldt and the soldiers who had defeated the Boers at Paardeberg were basking in the plaudits of the nation. Some of the original members of the Field Force were among those distinguishing themselves overseas, and the purpose, origin and function of the Yukon Field Force were all fading into the past, rarely to be contemplated again.

Edward Lester

The foundation of this book is the diary of Edward Lester, an English immigrant who served in the Force as a private soldier. The re-appearance of his diary, buried in the detritus of Fort Selkirk for twenty-five years and then held for fifty-five more in private hands in England — a history explained later — offered an opportunity to tell the story pretty well in the words of men and women who either served in the Field Force, or travelled with it. That part of the narrative which does not come from them is taken from the reminiscences of a French aristocrat, a tourist on his way to the Klondike out of sheer curiosity, who, by purest chance, was also a passenger on the ships that carried the Force first from Vancouver to Wrangell and then to Glenora, where the overland march began. What subsequently happened to some of these key figures in this story — a matter of character and circumstance — I have reconstructed from official records and newspapers.

Despite his obvious education and middle-class background, Lester himself presents us with a typical Victorian ranker's perspective (with his enthusiasms and prejudices), in which events often happen without apparent cause or necessary result. Why is the Force held so long at Glenora? If Lester knows, his knowledge is not displayed in the diary. Only when his pride is hurt, or the issue adversely affects his personal comfort or convenience, is he interested in causes. Fortunately, we have the official reports and correspondence of his commanding officer, Colonel Evans, to explain the causes and the consequences.

While Evans' olympian despatches detail cause, event, and result in spare, laconic prose, unencumbered with human interest· Lester gives us a sometimes thoughtful, always lively, worm's eye view of life in camp, on the trail, and on the boat trip down the Teslin and Yukon rivers. There are splendid descriptions of the scenery (perhaps most notably in a succinct recollection of the *aurora borealis* on the night of 5/6 April 1899, when he was up all night nursing a NWMP corporal recuperating from an attempt to cut his own throat), wry glimpses of his fellow-troopers and critical comments on the idiosyncrasies of his officers and the various Indians that he came across. There is even — amazingly enough at a time when so many scientists were proclaiming the imminent millennium when man would finally master nature — a stricture on the desperate need for environmental conservation!

As far as the march north is concerned, there are despatches from the *Toronto Globe*, mostly the work of their own, paid, female correspondent, but supplemented by one from a nurse who accompanied the advance party. Many of the photographs are the work of Henry Joseph Woodside, entrepreneur, one-time militia officer, and pioneer photo-journalist. Woodside, who knew Colonel Evans and possibly other officers of the Field Force, was on the trail at the same time, on his way to Dawson to take up an appointment as editor of the *Yukon Sun*.

Once installed at Selkirk, the entries in Lester's diary begin to slowly fade away, from an absorbing record of garrison activities to an increasingly hum-drum recitation of weather, mail deliveries, and the succession of routine duties — guards and fatigues — that plainly reflects the unutterable boredom and monotony of a Yukon winter spent 300 kilometres from the bright, if tawdry, lights of Dawson. Some time the following spring, Lester finished an entry — we shall never know which day it was, or what it was about, for the harsh climate destroyed both the first and last entries before the diary was salvaged — stuffed the manuscript into a convenient niche in the rough log wall of his barrack-room, and never took it out again. Did he simply get tired of it, or was he ordered from Selkirk so suddenly that he had no time to retrieve it? We shall never know.

For our purposes, Lester's story began in January, 1895, when a personable, well-educated and unattached Englishman in his middle twenties, not long from the Mother Country and calling himself Edward Lincoln enrolled in the sparse ranks of the 60th 'Missisquoi' Volunteer Battalion of the Active Militia of Canada.[4]

We do not know why he joined. The 60th was a moribund rural corps with its headquarters in Clarenceville, PQ, and its six constituent companies distributed in neighbouring communities of the Eastern Townships. It was not noted for its martial spirit — three years later it would be disbanded as inadequate even by the dismal standards of the rural militia — and it entirely lacked the social cachet and 'clubby' atmosphere associated with such élite city corps as Montreal's Victoria Rifles or Toronto's Queen's Own.

Lincoln may well have had financial difficulties. Canada was in the throes of an economic recession and he seems to have had neither marketable skills nor influence, but he may have had previous militia experience with the Volunteer movement in Britain and seen a way of using that to solve the short-term problem of staying alive and well through a Canadian winter. Although there was no financial advantage in *joining* the militia (in a rural battalion like the 60th pay was a dollar a day — about the wage of a general labourer — to a maximum of twelve days per annum, earned at a summer camp, but the 60th had not been to camp for several years) once he was enrolled there was the possibility of pay, board and lodging while attending courses offered to selected militiamen at one of the Royal Schools of Instruction run by the Permanent Force.

It may be that our man also saw the Schools as a convenient way of establishing his new identity, for Lincoln was not his real name. He had been born a Lester, in Liverpool in 1861, but "on account of private family reasons"[5] which remain obscure (possibly involving the mysterious 'M' of his Yukon diary) he had chosen to start a new life in the colonies under a new name, a remittance man without a remittance.

Sometime in the late winter of 1894–95, armed with the necessary recommendation from his colonel made out in the name of Lincoln, Edward Lester entered the infantry 'Short Course' conducted at St. Johns, PQ, (now the site of *Le Collège militaire royal* and known as St. Jean) by the staff of No. 3 Depot, Royal Regiment of Canadian Infantry. The course lasted six weeks and Lester earned a Second Class, or "B" Certificate that qualified him to be a subaltern officer in the Non-Permanent Volunteer Militia.[6] His certificate would not ensure a commission, however. There were economic, social, and sometimes political, criteria to be taken into account which were much more important, and many a Volunteer officer did not have a certificate, while some of those who did, did not have a commission.

He was then accepted for the 'Long Course', of three months' duration, which would have theoretically qualified him to command a battalion, but before completing it he enlisted as a private soldier in the Permanent Force, signing on for the standard three-year engagement. He gave his name as Lincoln, his age as 34, his marital status as single, and his former occupation as "medical student", a claim which, surprising though it may have been, must have gained some validity from the coat-of-arms of Guy's Hospital, one of London's greatest teaching hospitals, tattooed on his right forearm.[7] (Guy's have no record of a student named Edward Lester. He may have been using a false name there, too, or perhaps he was an employee of the hospital — employee records no longer exist.) In return he was awarded RRCI Regimental No. 5068, given the usual issue of kit, assigned a bed and locker in a barrack room occupied by nineteen other men, and entered on the paylist as being entitled to the princely sum of forty cents a day for his services, less, of course, certain established deductions.

A warm bed and regular food no doubt had their advantages at the time, but life in the Permanent Force obviously left a good deal to be desired in the minds of many recruits. Desertion rates in the '90's were horrendous and the military found it almost impossible to retain trained men whose enlistments expired. For Canada's one thousand regular soldiers there was no pension. Pay was better in either the Mounted Police or the United States Army, both of which did have pension schemes. Five men out of every six were either undergoing recruit training or employed on routine guards or fatigues: stable and fire picquets, cleaning, kitchen work, cutting wood and clearing snow being the main ones; only the sixth man was involved directly in the primary task of the Permanent Force: training the Active Militia in the military essentials of his part-time trade.

The current General Officer Commanding the Militia, Major-General I.J.C. Herbert of the British Army, seconded to Canadian service, was doing his best to improve the conditions of his men but financial and political restraints were restricting his efforts. Despite a twenty percent cut in establishments — a result of the recession, which allowed the Force to get rid of some of its most unsuitable men in 1895 — the infantry component lost another twenty-five percent of its strength in the following year. Eighteen completed their engagements and chose not to re-enlist, nineteen purchased their discharge, and another nineteen deserted.[8]

Nevertheless, Lester found a niche at St. Johns which apparently left him contented, if not happy, among the seventy men stationed there. He won no promotion but was never charged with a major disciplinary offence and, if the diary is to be believed, only a very few minor ones. He was a good soldier and the low pay, coarse company and mind-numbing succession of 'duties' and fatigues seem to have left no benchmarks of frustration or bitterness on him.

What would have happened if his initial engagement had expired while he was still at St. Johns, we cannot tell. Perhaps he would have taken his discharge and, his new identity firmly established, gone west or south in search of a situation more in keeping with his upbringing and education. Perhaps he would have re-enlisted anyway. What little we know of him suggests that he was not the kind of man who 'made things happen'. Most of his actions were simply reactions to external stimuli. Within limits Edward Lester usually went with the tide of circumstance.

In this case the tide that swept him into re-enlisting was the decision of the Canadian government to send a detachment of the Permanent Force to the Yukon Territory, where it was to back up the North-West Mounted Police in maintaining law and order among the disparate, and often desperate, characters of a dozen nationalities who were stampeding to the Klondike in search of gold.

The Klondike

The Klondike was not a name bandied about very often before the gold rush began. The vast watershed of the upper Yukon — embracing an area more than four times that of present-day Ontario, five times that of British Columbia, with a population estimated to be no more than 10,000 or 11,000, nearly all of them Indians — had been simply a source of prime fur and the occasional convert to Christianity ever since the first Caucasians had moved in, over the Frances and Pelly rivers from Fort Halkett, on the Liard, in the 1840's. Fort Frances, on Frances Lake, was the first Hudson Bay Company post within what is now the Yukon Territory, built by Robert Campbell in 1842; Pelly Banks, just across the continental divide was added in 1845, and Fort Selkirk, at the junction of the Pelly and Lewes rivers, where the Yukon River then began, (after the turn of the century, the Lewes and its tributary, the Thirty Mile, were added to the Yukon) in 1848, both by Campbell. Selkirk, however, was attacked and looted in July 1852 — without loss of life on either side — by a band of Chilcat Indians from the Pacific coast, whose own trade with the Indians of the interior had been adversely affected by the HBC's activities. The Company promptly abandoned the site (which was not very profitable, anyway), and not until 1889 did another, private, trader re-establish a post there.

Approaching from the Mackenzie delta, another HBC man, John Bell, had reached the headwaters of the Rat River in 1842, crossing the height of land and travelling down another stream — which he modestly named the Bell — until it flowed into a larger river, which he called the Porcupine. Two years later, he followed the Porcupine down to its junction with an even greater river, to which he gave his version of the name used by the Indians he encountered there. He called it the Youcon, and there he built Fort Youcon, distinguished as being the westernmost post ever to fly the HBC flag. In fact, Fort Youcon or Yukon was so far west that it stood in Russian territory.

The Russians had long been moving up the Yukon river from its estuary on the Bering Strait, and, as early as 1824–25, they and the British had negotiated a common boundary to divide territory about which neither of them knew very much. The Russians, at the time, claimed everything west of the 139th meridian, a line which would have given them three-quarters of the gold-filled Klondike basin. However they were more interested in their southern boundary, which would mark the southern tip of the Alaskan 'panhandle'. The final agreement, gave them the Pacific littoral down to 54 degrees 40' North, while the British got a boundary along the 141st meridian. Subsequently, in 1867, the Russians sold their North American colony to the United States for the absurd sum of $7,200,000 which would have been even more absurd if Alaska's eastern boundary had run along the 139th meridian! The Americans, better organized than the Russians, quickly compelled the HBC to relinquish Fort Yukon and retreat to what was, by then, the Canadian side of the border.

Prospecting began in the Yukon during the early 1870s and 'colours' were panned from many of the rivers. There was often enough to whet a miner's appetite but rarely enough to fill his belly. Most prospectors were trappers and traders as well. Placer mining was, at best, a marginal proposition until in 1886, a promising strike was made on the Fortymile River, so called because it joined the Yukon forty miles [64 km] upstream from the international boundary, and a modest stampede developed. Soon there were, perhaps, five hundred men working the creeks and gravel bars of the upper Yukon, some turning a reasonable profit from their claims, others barely surviving and always moving on in search of better prospects. In 1894 Ottawa established a permanent presence with a North-West Mounted Police detachment at Fort Constantine, just below the mouth of the Fortymile, which maintained a rough and ready order and extracted customs duties on supplies coming by river steamer nearly 2,000 kilometres from St. Michael's at the mouth of the Yukon. Twenty 'Mounties' were considered enough to keep the Queen's peace and ensure that most, if not all, of the customs and excise regulations were obeyed.

Then, in August 1896, George Washington Carmack and his Indian friends, Skookum Jim and Tagish Charlie, made a formidable strike on Rabbit Creek, a tributary of the Klondike that was shortly to be re-named Bonanza. Obeying the unwritten law of prospectors everywhere, they spread the word, but by the time the value of their discoveries was confirmed, the river was frozen, winter had set in, and the Yukon was isolated from the outside world for the next eight months.[9]

The handful of men on the spot grew rich but it was not until June 1897, when the Alaska Commercial Company's steamship *Excelsior* docked in San Francisco, that the world at large heard the news. Jubilant miners, dressed in rags, staggered ashore under the weight of $750,000 in nuggets and dust. The next day the S.S. *Portland* arrived at Seattle with another $800,000 worth of gold on board and the Klondike stampede was on.

> The news that the telegraph is bringing the past few days of the wonderful things of Klondike, in the land of the midnight sun, has opened the flood-gates and a stream of humanity is pouring through Seattle and on to the golden Mecca of the north. It is a crowd at once strange, weird and picturesque. Some say it eclipses anything in the days of '49.[10]

On 26 July *The Times* of London, the world's most influential newspaper, ran several columns on the new discoveries (shortly it would be sending its own correspondent to the scene) and, two days later, the Colonial Office felt it appropriate to issue a formal warning that men should not start for the goldfields at once—the brief Yukon summer was too far advanced — but should wait until the following spring. By 10 August the United States Department of the Interior was also warning people against attempting to reach the Klondike that year.[11] Nevertheless, about 700 adventurers did get in over the White and Chilcoot Passes from Skagway in 1897. A tent and shanty town arose on the gravel flat at the mouth of the Klondike, soon named Dawson in honour of Dr. George Mercer Dawson, of the Geological Survey of Canada, who had examined part of the upper Yukon basin in 1887 and predicted that major discoveries of gold might occur "at any time".[12]

The sudden influx of ill-prepared adventurers taxed the NWMP contingent to its limit. Ottawa reinforced them in several increments, as and when it could, and by the turn of the year there were 162 of them, including special constables and dog-team drivers. Over the winter nobody actually starved, and there was no breaking of the social fabric, such as it was. There were food shortages and scurvy, a disease caused by lack of fresh food. However, it was clear that the problems would be far worse in 1898. No one could really know how many would come, and guesses were no more than that. In the event, there would be not less than 30,000 entering the territory and the situation would only be saved by an arbitrary police decision not to allow anyone over the passes who was not bringing a year's supplies in with him. Dawson, the shanty town, would become Dawson, the shanty city.

The government in Ottawa had had some warning of what was likely to happen through the reports of William Ogilvie, a Dominion civil servant who was surveying the Alaska boundary when the first great strike was made. As a result those extra 'Mounties' had been available when needed, and John Morrow Walsh (the former inspector of the NWMP who had made his reputation by his handling of the Sioux Indians when Sitting Bull brought his people over the border after massacring General Custer and his 7th Cavalry at the Little Big Horn in 1876) had been lured back from the business world to accept an appointment as first Commissioner of the Yukon. At the end of January 1898 the redoubtable Superintendent Sam Steele was ordered north with another seventy 'Mounties', all that could be spared, bringing the total to 232. Recruiting of new constables forged ahead but, at the same time, a considerable proportion of those men whose engagements were expiring while they were in the Yukon were finding the advantages of civil life in a booming economy exceedingly attractive. As prospectors, they might even strike it rich themselves.

The Yukon Field Force

A month or so earlier the government had opened negotiations with the great civil engineering firm of Mackenzie and Mann to build a narrow-gauge railway into the Territory. The administration agreed to grant 25,000 acres [10,000 hectares] of land, with a border on the right-of-way, for every mile [1.6 kilometres] of track built. Because of the need for haste a contract was signed on 25

January, while parliament was still enjoying the Christmas break, in the hope that rail communication between Glenora, at the head of navigation on the Stikine river, and Teslin Lake, 232 kilometres [145 miles] to the north, on the headwaters of a tributary of the upper Yukon, could be established by September.

When parliament resumed sitting in February, the opposition found the terms of the contract excessively generous and suspected Liberal Party chicanery. In a heated debate over the Yukon Railway Bill, which would have ratified the contract, the idea of sending troops to the Territory first arose. One of the government's justifications for the precipitate signing of the contract was that the railway would be "vital if there should be a breakdown of law and order in the territory". That argument was resisted by the member for North York, N.C. Wallace, who held that the Mounted Police were quite capable of ensuring that that did not happen. However, he added, "I think it quite a proper safeguard to send a force to the Yukon Territory, a moderate force" which might discourage the United States from making any move to annex the area. Without giving any specific reason, Wallace feared that:

> They wanted to get a military foothold, they wanted to get some sort of possession of our Canadian territory. We know what their dealings with Canadian and British people have been. They get a foothold here and a foothold there, and once they get possession it is extremely hard to dislodge them.

The Minister of the Interior, Clifford Sifton, who had played a major part in the railway negotiations, poured contempt on the idea that the United States was after the Yukon, while explicitly admitting that there was a threat posed by the number of Americans in the territory. Without the railway he anticipated a winter (of 1898–99) in which:

> We would have to face the fact that 200 or 300 of our officers would be surrounded by starving thousands of armed men, of alien men, not citizens of Canada, but citizens of foreign countries, and these men would have possession of the Yukon district instead of the Government of Canada ... .We have before us the great danger of the authority of this government being over-ridden, being destroyed, and the Government of

that district being, theoretically, if not actually, taken out of our hands. [13]

A Liberal majority carried the bill through the Commons and it went to the Senate, where there was no telling what a Conservative majority might do with it. If it did not pass the Upper House, then Sifton's vision might well come true and, faced with that nightmare prospect, the administration began to develop Wallace's idea of sending troops to the Yukon. On 10 March the Prime Minister was asked if the rumour of a Field Force being sent there was correct, and Sir Wilfrid Laurier replied that "a small corps is being prepared at the present time to be sent out at the earliest moment". He was unable to say, just then, how the force would be constituted or how it would get there.[14]

On 21 March an Order-in-Council established that "a Field Force composed of volunteers from the permanent troops of the Dominion should be despatched to Fort Selkirk".[15] However, the matter was not put before the House of Commons until 4 May, when Dr. F.W. Borden, the Minister of Militia and Defence, outlined the reasons for the government's decisions on the composition of the force and the route it would take to the Yukon.

> At first, I believe, it was intended to increase the mounted police force, but on further consideration it was thought that it would better serve the objects in view to send a detachment of the permanent force, which would establish a central force in that country, would have a decided moral effect upon the scattered population throughout the district, and if necessity demanded would be ready to assist in enforcing law and maintaining order there .... In addition to the 200 members of the force, there will be a very few men who will go up as artificers and boatmen to assist in carrying the expedition.... I may say it is intended to send the troops by the Stikine River and overland from Glenora to Teslin Lake to Fort Selkirk. It is intended there to establish barracks, to construct certain defensive works, and to make the men as comfortable as possible ... They are armed with Lee-Enfield rifles; they will take two Maxim [machine-] guns and two seven-pound field guns.[16]

Borden did not fail to point out that since a soldier's pay was only half that of a Mounted Policeman's (both got double pay in the

Yukon) a military contingent would cost the taxpayer less than an equivalent number of police re-enforcements. Clearly the proposed Force was intended as a symbol of Canadian sovereignty. Only if "necessity demanded" would it be "ready to assist" in maintaining law and order, a duty for which "defensive works" and field guns were unlikely tools. But it would have a "decided moral effect upon the scattered population *throughout the district*" and it was probably this last phrase that dictated the choice of Fort Selkirk, rather than Dawson, as the Force's base. Small strikes of gold were continually occurring over a wide area and there was no guarantee that the gold rush would be limited to the vicinity of Dawson. In 1898 there was only an Indian village at Selkirk, where, as we have noted an independent trader had established a small store in the early '90's. The only remnants of the old Fort Selkirk were several ruined stone chimneys, but the government was firmly committed to Selkirk as the eventual capital and just as determined that the Field Force should be based there despite Commissioner Walsh's arguments from Dawson that, if the Force was to be at his beck and call, it should properly be held close at hand, not 320 kilometres up the river. [17]

Creating a 200-man Field Force from Canada's miniscule regular army was not an administratively easy thing to do. A quarter of

PERMANENT
FORCE STATIONS
1898

the Permanent Force's strength was required, which would have to be raised by assigning quotas to the various corps, schools and depots, with only the cavalry at Toronto — 'A' Squadron, Royal Canadian Dragoons — being left virtually untouched. Only volunteers were to go, "none but men absolutely sound in every way, capable of standing exceptional hardship are to be selected", and every man with "less than two years service unexpired will be required to re-engage for a new three-year term. [18]

In most of the depots — Winnipeg, London, Toronto, Kingston, St. Johns, Quebec and Fredericton — there was a surfeit of volunteers, although at Toronto the RRCI had to transfer one man from the RCD squadron there to make up their quota. Three officers and 146 men of the Royal Canadian Artillery, three officers and 130 men of the RRCI (including Edward Lester, whose engagement had been due to expire in August), and one officer and sixteen men of the RCD were picked for the body of the Force, together with a headquarters staff of five additional officers.

Command of the Force went to Major (promoted to acting Lieutenant-Colonel for the duty) Thomas D.B. Evans, who had commanded 'B' Squadron, RCD, stationed at Winnipeg, for the previous three years. Evans had earlier been selected to lead the cavalry contingent to London for Queen Victoria's Diamond Jubilee, and had just been appointed an Honorary Aide-de-Camp

Lieut–Col. Thomas B.D. Evans, commanded the Yukon Police Force

23

to the Governor-General, Lord Aberdeen. In the Canadian context he was uniquely qualified to command a mixed force of gunners, horse soldiers and infantrymen. Beginning his career in the ranks, he had earned a First Class certificate and been commissioned into the 43rd 'Ottawa and Carleton Rifles' Battalion of the Volunteer Militia in 1881 at the age of 21. He was soon promoted to a captaincy and made adjutant of the unit in 1884, having demonstrated "a marked capacity for command and a decided ability in begetting enthusiasm in his men."[19]

Not short of enthusiasm himself, Evans had also earned First Class certificates from schools of cavalry and artillery, which meant that he was qualified to command a regiment of either, as well as an infantry battalion. In 1885 he had managed to get himself included in the composite 'Midland' Battalion of the Active Militia, which was formed for service in the North-West Rebellion and played a major part at Fish Creek and Batoche.

In 1888 he was gazetted into the Permanent Force as a lieutenant, in what was then the Infantry School Corps and later became the RRCI. Sent to England, to the School of Musketry at Hythe, he had again distinguished himself. In 1891 he had been transferred to the School of Mounted Infantry at Winnipeg and subsequently had attended mounted infantry and veterinary schools in England, achieving his customary standards of excellence.[20]

Evans' commanding officer at Winnipeg, a 'society' soldier who had no command talent and little feeling for the men, owed his position to the patronage of a former Minister of Militia, Sir Adolphe Caron. In 1895, three years after Caron left office, his abuse of the squadron had brought about a minor mutiny.[21]After the usual formal 'whitewash' he had been posted back to the regiment's headquarters in Toronto, in a subordinate appointment where he could do less harm, and Evans had been promoted to take his place and had improved conditions, restored discipline and built up morale in short order. There was no better, or better-qualified officer in Canada.

Finding officers, however, proved more of a problem than finding men, perhaps because, when the headquarters complement was included, the proportion of commissioned ranks needed was significantly greater. On Evans' staff went Captain E.W.E.

Gardiner (who had been commissioned from the ranks) as his adjutant, with Sergeant-Major J.R. Young as his regimental sergeant-major. Both of them were from his own squadron of the RCD. Major D.D. Young, who had been commissioned into the Infantry School Corps when a permanent infantry component had first been established, was appointed second-in-command. Major Aimé Talbot of the 9th 'Voltigeurs de Québec' Volunteer Battalion was made paymaster, Surgeon-Major G. LaF. Foster of the 68th 'Kentville' Battalion was the medical officer, and Major D.C.F. Bliss of the Reserve of Officers became quartermaster, responsible for all supplies and transportation arrangements.

Bliss, who had once been a ranker in the Permanent Force artillery, had also served as a subaltern in the 'Midland' Battalion during the North-West campaign. When he was called out for service with the Field Force he was a civil servant with the Department of Militia and Defence. Talbot, too, had been in the North-West. Gilbert Foster, however, had only joined the Active Militia (as a newly-qualified doctor from McGill) in August 1897.

With two exceptions the line officers were career regulars from the Permanent Force, several of them being given an acting rank one level above their regular one: Captains J.H.C. Ogilvie (Lester consistently spells it with a 'y') and H.E. Burstall of the RCA; P.E. Thacker of the RRCI and C. St. A. Pearse of the RCD. Thacker, born in 1871, graduated from the Royal Military College at Kingston in 1894, and gazetted into the infantry the following year, was both the youngest and most junior of them.

The two exceptions were Captain L.G. Bennett, identified as belonging to the 'Engineer Reserve' at Halifax, and Lieutenant Louis Leduc of the 65th Volunteer Battalion, both of whom were granted permanent commissions for the occasion, Bennett in the artillery and Leduc in the infantry. There was no Canadian Corps of Engineers until 1903 and Bennett's professional skills may have accounted for his selection. Leduc's case was apparently one of patronage, for among the Volunteer Militia many applied but few were chosen — by the Minister personally, if the General Officer Commanding the Militia is to be believed. [22]

The Klondike lay further north than any formed body of Canadian troops — or Imperial troops, for that matter — had ever served before. Queen Victoria's soldiers and their predecessors had won her dominion over palm and pine from Vancouver Island to Hong Kong, and south to Tasmania and the Falkland Islands, but the previous 'farthest north' seems to have been in the vicinity of Frenchman's Butte during the North-West Rebellion. That had been a summer campaign; the Yukon Field Force would be operating ten degrees of latitude further north on a year-round basis.

> It was immediately apparent that the kitting and equipping of the Force would be no simple matter. For the first time the Canadian defence establishment was forced to consider the single most important characteristic of the north: isolation. In the Yukon there were no established sources of services and supply.... The Force would have to be prepared to operate self-sufficiently once it was in the Yukon .... Even such a mundane item as uniforms presented problems, for not only did the troops require their regular field and garrison dress, but they also needed a durable fatigue uniform and special environmental clothing that would allow them to face the rigours of winter.[23]

Colonel Percy Lake, the quartermaster-general, and his staff turned to the task with a will. By 19 March a Winnipeg newspaper was reporting that "All the men have been measured for winter clothing, which will comprise canvas trousers and jackets, Dolge felts (winter boots), moccasins with fur inside, duffles, special mitts, caps, working linen suits, etc."[24] The list of supplies was immense, including 300 rounds of ammunition for each rifle, 25,000 rounds for the Maxim guns and 200 rounds for the two seven-pounders. Ration staples included 40,000 kg of tinned meats, 20,000 kg of 'hard tack' biscuits, and 63,000 kg of flour, to a total value of $30,000. Most of it was purchased from established government contractors without going out to tender, since time was of the essence — a procedure which quickly brought some stiff parliamentary questioning by the opposition.[25]

Nevertheless, by 6 May 1898 everything was ready and all except the Winnipeg contingent had concentrated at Ottawa, anxious to be off. The previous day they had been inspected and commended by the Prime Minister; that morning it was the Governor-General's turn. But eventually the formalities were over and, at precisely eleven o'clock, the great oaken doors of the Ottawa Drill Hall (still standing on Cartier Square, though the doors are no longer oak) swung open and some 190 officers and men marched out into the sunshine led by the band of the Governor-General's Foot Guards. The streets to the station, where a special train was waiting to carry them west, were lined with cheering spectators and envious small boys, wishing that they could go along. At the station the band played them off with a spirited rendering of "The Girl I Left Behind Me",²⁶ a tune which may well have had peculiar associations for Edward Lester.

Two days later the train pulled into Winnipeg to pick up the sixteen-man contingent from the RCD. "The men are a handsome lot of fellows without exception," enthused one reporter, "being tall, strongly built, and of very soldierly appearance, and undoubtedly the finest lot of men ever seen in Her Majesty's uniform here". The people of Winnipeg spared no effort to provide a memorable stopover for the troops.

> Mr. E.L. Drewry, with his usual generosity, has promised to look after the soldiers' beverages; Messrs. Brown and Co. will provide the soothing weed; Mr. Boyd will see that the staff of life is not neglected; Mr. J.C. Hargrove and Capt. Adams of the Hudson's Bay Co. are determined that

The Royal Canadian Dragoons' contingent of the Field Force, photographed before leaving Winnipeg

the inner man will have no feeling of regret at visiting
Winnipeg, and Messrs. Blackwood Bros. have the special
care of the prohibitionists of the party.

History does not record how the prohibitionists made out, but Mr.
Drewry's success was attested to by the pleasant fact that "the
fountain of beer never ran dry."[27]
Late that evening the whole Force, including the Dragoons,
marched — or lurched — back to the train. No doubt there were
some sore heads the next morning, but all was well when they
reached Vancouver on 11 May. The men were bedded down in a
disused theatre, while the officers were lodged in a nearby hotel.
In Vancouver the Force formally linked up with the civilians who
were to accompany them into the Yukon — eleven employees of
the Department of the Interior, bound for technical and administrative posts in Dawson, and six women.

The Feminine Contingent
Four of the women were members of the Victorian Order of
Nurses, an organization founded only a year earlier under the
patronage of the Governor General's wife, to provide trained
nursing care in remote areas. At that time the Order had met with
considerable resistance, not only from the media and the public,
but from the medical profession itself. In the gold rush Lady
Aberdeen saw a golden opportunity to swing all three behind her
new Order; nowhere could be more remote or more likely to need
nurses than the Yukon, and nowhere would success be assured of
more publicity.
She carefully selected four nurses sure to do the Order credit
and wrote to the *Toronto Globe* about them — "Miss Powell, a lady
from Nova Scotia who will be in command of the Expedition; Miss
Payson from New Brunswick; Miss Hanna from Toronto; and Miss
Scott who came out from Great Britain a few years ago...." (Actually, Georgia Powell was from Buctouche, NB, Margaret Payson
was from Weymouth, NS, and Rachel Hanna was from Port
Carling, Ont.).

All these ladies are fully trained nurses of great experience
and have splendid testimonials from leading physicians under

28

whom they have worked. They are fully aware of the hardships which they will have to face.... The Government has decided to send our nurses forward under the care of the detachment of troops which is to start about the end of April, and the present plan is that they accompany them all the way to Fort Selkirk, the probable capital of the district. ...By this excellent arrangement, we are assured of the nurses' safety *en route,* and we hope that, in this way, there will be as little delay as possible in their getting to work.[28]

Five of the six women who took the Klondike Trail in 1898: Georgia Powell (Buctouche, N.B.), Amy Scott (England), Rachel Hanna (Port Carling, Ont.), Margaret Payson (Weymouth, N.S.) and Faith Fenton (*Toronto Globe*)

Making quite sure that the participation of the nurses was kept in the public eye, three weeks later Lady Aberdeen entertained them at Rideau Hall.

After dinner an informal reception was held in the ballroom. Samples of their outfits were on exhibition. On a lay figure was exhibited a sample of their neat brown duck suits, made with a short skirt with bloomers and gaiters in the style of a natty bicycle suit, which they will wear when they walk those long, long 150 miles over mountain and swamp.

On another figure their waterproof suits and tarpaulin hats were shown, and there was also on a third figure their winter suit of heavy blue blanket, with a big hood to match, lined with quilted silk.

Perhaps the sleeping bags were those items which were most minutely examined. They are made of canvas lined with flannel and interlined with eiderdown .... It was rather fun to listen to the varied criticisms that were made of the various articles in the outfit. This one knew quite well that the sleeping bag would never keep them warm, and that one thought that the boots should not have had nails in the soles, as it made them more likely to slip on the rocks; another did not see how women could walk in such heavy boots at all. After some time had been spent in inspection, His Excellency, in Her Majesty's name, accepted the nurses into the Victorian Order and clasped a jubilee ribbon and silver medal about their necks.[29]

The addition of four nurses to the Field Force apparently fired the imagination of the *Toronto Globe's* editor, who now sought and received permission to send a female correspondent along. His candidate was Faith Freeman, who wrote under the name of Fenton, a Toronto woman who had already made a reputation for herself on the *Empire*, a *Globe* competitor, with a feature series about the isolated lighthouses of Canada, many of which she had actually visited.[30] Lastly, and probably quite unofficially, the French-Canadian wife of Inspector Cortlandt Starnes of the NWMP, had managed to attach herself to the Force for the journey north to join her husband. Given the mores of the time, she, of course, could act as chaperone to the group.

The Journey North

From Vancouver there were four feasible routes into the Yukon in 1898. The easiest, but longest and most time-consuming, was by ocean-going steamship 4,000 kilometres across the North Pacific, threading through the Aleutian chain of islands, to St. Michael's, on the Bering Sea's Norton Sound where the Yukon River debouched into the sea. From St. Michael's passengers and freight had to be transferred to flat-bottomed river steamers and then travel another 2,700 kilometres upstream to Dawson.

For the Field Force there were two problems with that route. It was questionable whether it could reach its destination before the

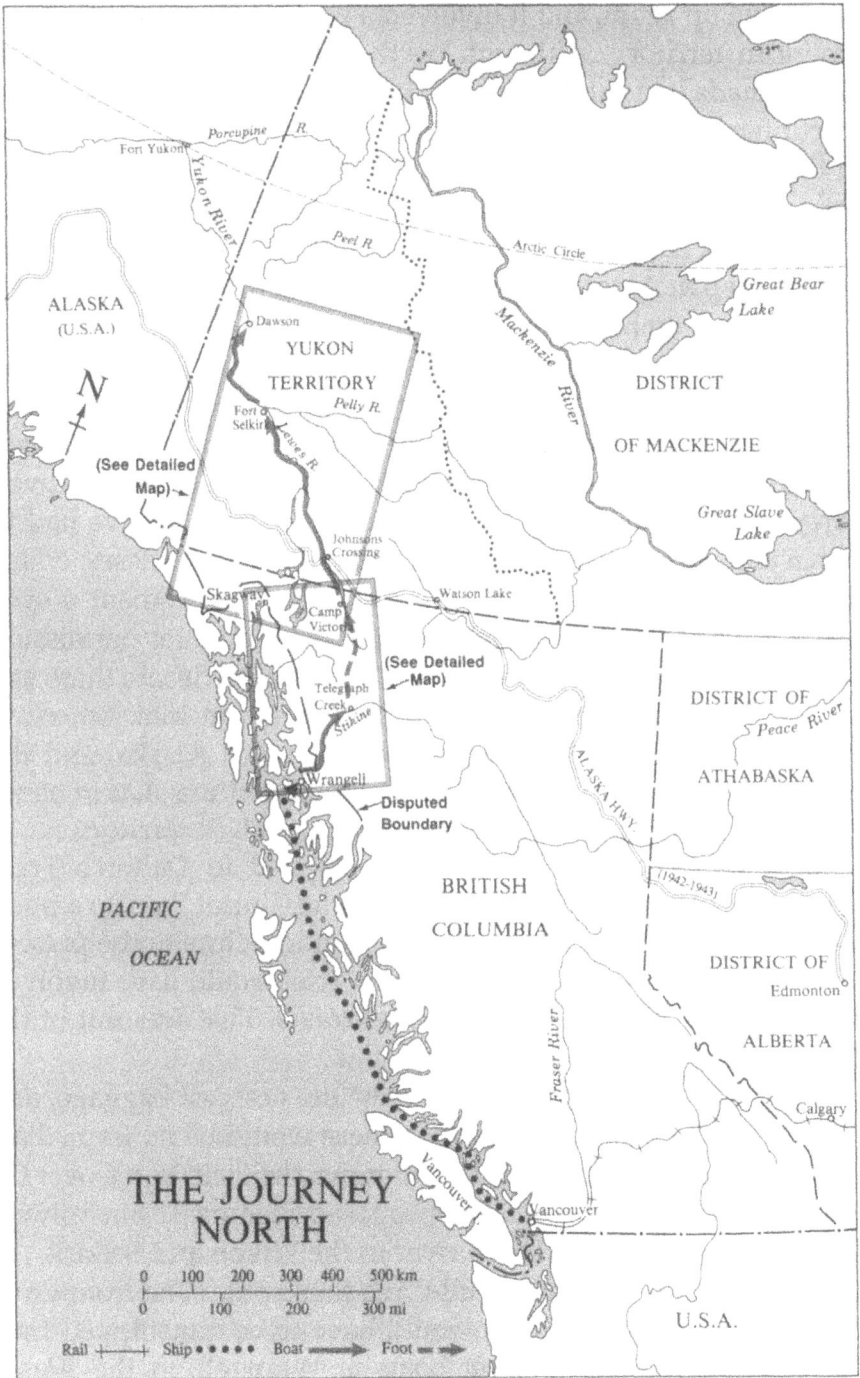

THE JOURNEY
NORTH

| Rail +——+ | Ship ••••• | Boat ——→ | Foot ━━▶ |

river froze up again, and it involved a prolonged voyage through American territory. Although by the Treaty of Washington, in 1871, Canada had gained the right of free navigation on the Yukon, Porcupine and Stikine rivers in exchange for American privileges on the St. Lawrence, the government was reluctant to commit its troops to an access route so demonstrably American. Moreover, what would happen if, through some mischance, the Force was caught deep in American territory by 'freeze-up' and the onset of winter? How embarrassing that would be.

The shortest, quickest and most popular ways into the Yukon were through Dyea or Skagway, over the Chilcoot or White passes that pierced the barrier of coastal mountains, and then down through a chain of lakes to the upper reaches of the Yukon River. Carrying or pulling their weapons, the men would have had to march across the coastal strip, from the ports to the passes, which was American territory; and the Canadian government would have had to make a formal request to Washington for permission for them to do so. During the Yukon Railway Bill debate there had been loudly-voiced objections to the suggestion that American troops might use a Canadian railway to reach Alaska, and the government could hardly now go to the Americans, hat in hand, for permission to march armed men through U.S. territory.

Exactly the same disadvantages applied to Dalton's Trail, which led from Pyramid Harbour over the Chilcat Pass, to a point on the upper Yukon near Five Finger Rapids, close to the present town of Carmacks. However, Dalton's Trail would have involved much more marching and less water travel. That was out of the question, given the Force's logistic 'tail'.

The fourth alternative was to have the heaviest baggage, and that part of the supplies for which there would be no immediate need, shipped via St. Michael's and move the Field Force over the touted 'all-Canadian' line of the proposed Glenora-Teslin railway, then by boat down the Teslin river to the Yukon and Selkirk.

It was not, of course, an 'all-Canadian' route. The troops and everything going with them would have to be transhipped from ocean-going steamer to river boats at Wrangell, in the Alaska 'panhandle', and then floated over American territorial waters into the Stikine river. But the Stikine was one of those rivers on which the Canadians had been guaranteed navigation rights and the men would not necessarily have to set foot on American soil. In pursuit of the government's "insane desire ... to find an all-Canadian route" even though "none of the new maps agree where the trail is"[31], it was decided that this was the way the Force should go. Accordingly, a hundred tons of supplies and equipment (including the two obsolete seven-pounder field guns, broken down into their component parts) were shipped in bond the long way round, while eighty tons of essentials, the troops and their civilian 'camp-followers', were all loaded aboard the Canadian Pacific's *S.S. Islander* for the run up the British Columbia coast and the southern third of the 'panhandle' to Wrangell. The *Islander* left Vancouver on 14 May.

It was probably at this point that Edward Lester began to keep a diary. The first twenty-five pages of it are missing, apparently having disintegrated in the harsh environment it was subjected to during those first twenty years after Lester laid it aside at Fort Selkirk. However, we can make up this part of the story very well from other first-person accounts.

Colonel Evans reported that the arrangements on board the *Islander* were "very unsatisfactory. Bunks reserved for the Force occupied by civilians, thereby causing delay on arrival at the steamer".[32] It may have taken a while but he did not hesitate to have the male passengers turned out where necessary so that some members of his party — probably the women-folk and officers — could get the accommodation that had been reserved for them. Among those to lose their cabin accommodation was a French gentlemen, M. Loicq du Lobel, and his two sons. Du Lobel and his family were on a sight-seeing jaunt to the goldfields and he subsequently published a memoir of their adventure. In French, he wrote that:

> On 14 May we embarked on the *Islander*, with my wife, my two daughters and my two sons, who would not consent to await my return to Vancouver. Our apprenticeship to the rough existence that we were going to lead for the next six months began here. This tiny steamship was occupied by 250 soldiers of the Yukon militia. As there were only enough reserved cabins for the ladies, we slept on the bridge ... .

> We arrived at Wrangel on 17 May. Wrangel is a small town built entirely of wood and raised on piles, but well-sited on a wooded hill .... The streets are immense ditches, real cesspools of dirt and street-sweepings of every kind; here and there emerge the trunks of trees sawn off a meter above ground and supporting rotten planks which bend under the feet. These sidewalks are very narrow and one can only walk on them with caution.
>
> It rains at Wrangel all the year round, I am told. As recently as 1897 Wrangel was an Indian village with only three whites. Now the larger part of the population is white and very bad. It is dangerous to be out after 7 o'clock at night when the days are short; they take your life there for 4 bits. Consciences, I am told, are bought and sold for from five to ten dollars; those of magistrates, however, are rated a little higher.[33]

Sam Steele, who had called in there on his way north, four months earlier, had also marked Wrangell down as "a mean and squalid spot with the usual number of gambling dens and other low dives."[34] Nurse Georgina Powell simply noted that "A big crowd gathered at the wharf to meet the boat. It was raining and Wrangel did not look inviting."[35]

It was at Wrangell that Colonel Evans met and overcame the first real emergency of the expedition. Here, at the beginning of the wilderness, Faith Fenton appeared in her travelling dress, shorter than the fashions of the time decreed and without the bloomers and gaiters that made the dresses of the nurses acceptable. Horrified, and fearing the effect of a well-turned ankle on the morals of his gallant men, the bachelor colonel deputed Mrs. Starnes to speak to her. Somewhere in Wrangell Starnes and Fenton found a fabric store and the latter's dress was soon made respectable by a modest band of black sateen tacked on to the hem. [36] Thus the innocent soldiery were secured from temptation, and no doubt Colonel Evans slept well that night, conscious of a duty well done.

Although the officers and civilians certainly went ashore, it is far from clear whether any of the other ranks were allowed off the *Islander*. R.C. Fetherstonhaugh (who had access to the diary of another member of the Force, Private F.H. Freeland, which can not now be located) claimed, when he wrote his history of the Royal Canadian Regiment in the early 1930s, that "the Force was welcomed by officers and the coloured other ranks of a detachment of United States infantry" in garrison there. But he also records how it took two days to transfer all the stores to the paddlewheel steamers, *Strathcona* and *Stikine Chief*, which were to carry them up the Stikine. "Only one mishap occurred when, due to the breaking of a sling, the Force's two-year supply of coffee fell into the sea and sank in fourteen fathoms of water,"[37] a depth which makes it certain that the transshipment was not carried out while alongside a wharf. Since they had to act as their own stevedores, the men must have spent most of their time on board. Given the problems of boating them ashore and ensuring that they got into no trouble once they were there, it seems likely that most of them saw nothing of Wrangell at close quarters.

The two river steamers left Wrangell together about 10 a.m. on 19 May. The *Stikine Chief* promptly ran aground on a sandbar off the mouth of the Stikine and the *Strathcona*, carrying Edward Lester and the Du Lobels, slipped into the lead. A few hours later she steamed past the invisible line that marked the limit of United States territory and entered Canadian waters, driving steadily upstream against the powerful current. Sometime that afternoon or early evening, Edward Lester pencilled the first surviving entry in the diary that would record his actions and impressions during the next thirteen months.

END NOTES

1. Quoted by Stephen Usherwood in "From Our Own Correspondent: Flora Shaw on the Klondike", *History Today*, (July, 1977), p. 451.
2. Walsh to Clifford Sifton, 6 March 1898, in Sifton Papers, PAC, MG 27, II, D 15, Vol. 295.
3. Officer Commanding Yukon Force to Adjutant-General, 1 November 1898, in Directorate of History, NDHQ, 73/78.
4. Edward Lester to the Board of Pension Commissioners, 28 September 1920, in Public Archives of Canada, reference file 1536.
5. *Ibid.*
6. *Ibid.*
7. Register of Enlistments, RCR Archives, Wolseley Barracks, CFB London, Ont. Canada, Department of Militia and Defence, *Militia Report*, 1896.
8. See Allen A. Wright, *Prelude to Bonanza: The Discovery and Exploration of the Yukon* (Sidney, BC, 1976) for an excellent account of the early history of the territory.
9. Quoted in E.T. Adney, *The Klondike Stampede of 1897-1898* (New York, 1900), pp. 4-5. This is probably the best first-person account of the Yukon gold rush.
10. Stephen Usherwood, "From Our Own Correspondent: Flora Shaw on the Klondike" in *History Today* (July, 1977), p. 445.

11. Adney, *loc. cit.*,p 8. See also Pierre Berton, *Klondike: The Life and Death of the Last Gold Rush* (Toronto, 1958).

12. George M. Dawson, *Report on an Exploration in the Yukon District, N.W.T....* (Ottawa, 1887), p. 23.

13. Canada, House of Commons, *Debates*, 8 February 1898.

14. *Ibid.*

15. *Militia Report*, 1898.

16. House of Commons, *Debates*, 4 May 1898.

17. Walsh to Sifton, 18 April, 23 June, 7, 23 and 24 July 1898, in Sifton Papers, Public Archives of Canada, MG 27, II, d 15, vol. 295.

18. Adjutant-General to Officer Commanding, No. 4 Regimental Depot, RRCI, 14 March 1898, in PAC, RG 9, II, B 1, Vol. 595.

19. *Manitoba Free Press*, 21 August 1908.

20. *Ibid.*

21. *Manitoba Morning Free Press*, 13 August 1895. See also GOC (Herbert) to Adjutant-General, 5 November 1883, in Royal Canadian Dragoons Archive, CFB Gagetown, N.B. for a critique of the low standards prevailing in Winnipeg.

22. PAC, RG 9 II, B 1, Vol. 280, f. 77013. Biographical material from *Militia Lists*, 1883-98; Jackson lists and biogaphical files in Directorate of History, National Defence Headquarters, Ottawa; and personal documents, Public Archives Record Centre.

23. K.C. Eyre, "Custos Borealis: The Military in the Canadian North". unpublished Ph. D. thesis, King's College, London, England. pp. 25-6.

24. *Winnipeg Daily Tribune*, 19 March 1898.

25. PAC, RG 9, II, a 1, f. 71958, and *Debates*, 4 June 1898, cols. 7060-62.

26. *Ottawa Evening Citizen*, 6 May 1898.

27. *Manitoba Morning Free Press*, 9 May 1898.

28. *Toronto Globe*, 28 March 1898.

29. *Ibid.*, 19 April 1898.

30. Obituary notice, *Toronto Globe*, 11 January 1936.

31. Adney, *loc. cit.*, p 17.

32. Evans to Adjutant-General, 1 November 1898 in D Hist 73/78.

33. Loicq du Lobel, *Le Klondyke, l'Alaska, le Yukon, et les iles Aleoutiennes*, (Paris, 1899), pp 5-6.

34. Steele, *loc. cit.*, p 292.

35. *Toronto Globe*, 1 October 1898.

36. Lucile Labelle, *Aux avant-postes du Canada: Sous le signe du bison*, (Montreal, 1962), p 51.

37. R. C. Fetherstonhaugh, *The Royal Canadian Regiment, 1883-1933*, (Montreal, 1936), p 68.

ARCHIVAL DETECTIVE WORK
THE PROVENANCE OF THE LESTER DIARY

by Gerald G. Cumming[1]

In July, 1981 a document described as the "manuscript diary of an unknown member of the Yukon Field Force" was placed on my desk in the Manuscript Division of the Public Archives of Canada. It had been forwarded from the Archives office in London, England and it was a document that I had been awaiting with some curiosity and enthusiasm. About a year earlier our London office had been informed by the Midland Bank Trust Company, acting as executors for the estate of the late Miss Florence Annie Taylor of Ditton Close, Thames Ditton, Surrey, that the dear lady had willed the diary to Canada's Public Archives.

What connection the late Miss Taylor had with the Yukon Field Force, if any, was unstated. How the diary had come into her possession was unknown. Perhaps some answers could be obtained from the executors. However, the onset of a Canadian postal strike prevented me from obtaining answers from those sources at that time.

The diary eventually arrived at my desk in the same brown envelope used by the Midland Bank Trust Company and perhaps by the donor herself. It was the envelope which seemed to provide an easy answer as to how Miss Taylor acquired the diary. Written in longhand across the front of the envelope was the notation "Yukon Field Force Diary found in the old barracks at Fort Selkirk by Florence Taylor (probably in 1919)". The diary had been in her custody for sixty years! Perhaps many times during those sixty years she pondered the question that now intrigued me - who wrote the diary? The answer to that question would not only satisfy my own deep-seated curiosity but most important it would go a long way towards authentication of the diary, a vital matter from the archival point of view.

The document which emerged from the envelope was in appalling condition. It was extremely fragile to the touch; the binding

37

7 June 9ᵗʰ Last night we slept in the open air rolled in our blankets. We having been strengthened by 3 more men & issued with loose ball ammunition with orders to shoot if necessary. We dismounted at 9.30 a.m. and marched up to the camp by a very steep & rough waggon road. The camp is picturesquely situated on two flats overlooking the creek on the opposite side to the road. No 1 Co⁷ are on the first flat & Nos 2 & 3 on the flat or terrace above so that we can look down into No 1 Coy's lines about 200 ft below us; the descent is so precipitous that the road from one level to the other has to be zigzagged. The kitchens are at the bottom of the valley on the banks of the creek of which the water is very clear & very cold. Opposite the Camp & by the road side are the Q.M. Stores & here the quarter-guard is mounted. Both Companies are on fatigue passing boxes & bales up from the wharf to the camp with the chaps which were issued at Glenora & which by the bye are known as "hump lines". There was a fatigue from 6 to 8 p.m. Mailed letters to Cotton & home

Fri June 1ᵗʰ Reveille at 4 a.m. Breakfast at 4.45 fall in for Fatigue at 5 a.m. Passing up the stores till 9.0. a.m. We are getting 4 meals a day & double working pay whilst we are getting the stores up. No work during the heat of the day Started again at 6 p.m. & worked till 8 p.m. Supper at 8.30. I feel as fit as a fiddler not a bit fagged. There are a lot of Indians in this place They belong to what is known as the "Siwash" Tribe & are not at all like the Indians of the western prairies. They say

had long ago been broken and many pages were brown with age, badly creased, torn and smudged with dirt. Before attempting to examine it I consigned it to the expert care of the Archives Conservation Division. Unnecessary handling before restoration would only have further damaged the already battered diary.

In approximately two weeks the diary was returned. The conservation experts had done their usual excellent job and the pages and binding had been cleaned, restored and strengthened for normal research use. Yet it was only then, after a thorough examination, that I realized how much of the manuscript had been lost over the years. Both front and back covers had disappeared and the first 24 pages and an indeterminate number of concluding pages were missing. As well, between the first and last entries, that is, 19 May 1898 and 27 April 1899, some 31 days were lost through damaged or missing entries. The historical information that perished with the lost pages was regrettable. The absence of a front cover struck me as particularly unfortunate in that diarists usually record their names on or inside diary covers. Whether that was so in this case we shall never know, but there was certainly no direct evidence of authorship on it in 1981.

Despite its mutilated condition, I hoped that clues to the diarist's identity lay somewhere among the faded diary pages. However, it soon became quite clear from the diarist's daily activities that he was not an officer or non-commissioned officer. He was one of the approximately 157 private soldiers who served with the Field Force. With this discovery my spirits sank for the task of identifying the author now appeared more difficult. Generally, historical information on commissioned officers in the old Canadian Militia is more abundant and accessible than information on enlisted men. Furthermore, even if I did discover his name, after eighty years the chance of unearthing enough biographical information about a private soldier in the Canadian Militia to really flesh out our diarist seemed improbable.

A survey of existing records on the Field Force available in the Public Archives soon brought the realization that the only body of documents which promised to yield any information on the enlisted men was the unit paylists. These lists have been preserved, along with thousands of other records of Canadian military history, in Record Group 9 of the Federal Archives Division.

The paylists grouped all the enlisted men of the Field Force into three companies. I reasoned that if I could first discover the company to which the diarist belonged, I would have at least narrowed the identity of the diarist to a group of about 50 rank and file. Then I hoped that other clues within the diary would allow me to isolate the author from his company comrades.

I began a careful reading of the diary from its beginning at page 25. As I read I began to compile a list of all the personal names mentioned by the author. I hoped that I could take the names, especially those with whom he seemed to associate on a daily basis, and relate them to the names found on the paylist of one of the companies.

The first few pages yielded tantalizing but hardly definitive clues:

> **2 June** ... The *Elwood* brought mail. I got a St. John's News from Cotton but no letter. Spence however got one from him... Bob Langille seems sick, he has been failing for some time... .
>
> **7 June** ... Lce. Corp. Grey (Fredericton) refused to fall in at all saying he was no d_____d pack mule ... .
>
> **8 June** ... Immediately after revielly [sic] this morning (5:30) we got the order. Turn out No. 3 at once in marching order... .

Clearly the last cited quotation pointed strongly to the diarist being a member of No. 3 Company. As well, the aforementioned individuals — Spence, Langille and Grey — were all found on No. 3 Company paylist for 1 to 30 June 1898.[2] I felt that these references represented good, but not conclusive evidence. I wanted the weight of a series of solid references before I would begin to look for clues pointing to an individual within a particular company.

Other references followed in rapid succession:

> **11 June** ... Issued with what is supposed to be a two months supply of tobacco, but through a mistake of Sgt. Lapierre's our section got only 4 plugs. I got two extra from Bobbie Graham...
>
> **12 June** ... I am for guard at 6 p.m. with Platt and Lowe...

> 13 June ... Platt, Lowe and I slept in the open rolled in out blankets... .

Almost all the soldiers mentioned in the above quotations were found on the No. 3 Company paylist for June 1898. Finally came the reference which confirmed the diarist's affiliation with No. 3 Company:

> 19 June ... Yesterday the vacancies in our tent caused by the men who have gone away with the ax party were filled. Corp. Hansen taking Corp. Hanlon's place. There are now in our tent Sgt. Lapierre, Corp. Hansen, Fowler, Platt, myself, Spence, Lefevbre, Dore, Graham, Hayes, McGowan and Lowe...

All the above mentioned men were found on the No. 3 Company June 1898 paylist. If the diarist's tent mates were from No. 3 Company, there could be little doubt about his own affiliation. Later references in the diary only served to confirm my conclusion.

But now, how to distinguish the mysterious diarist from the 54 other enlisted men in No. 3 Company? I continued my careful reading of each page, noting anything which could conceivably isolate the diarist from his comrades. As well, I continued to compile my list of all the names mentioned in the text. There was a chance that if the evidence I gathered pointed to more than one soldier in the company, my list of names could prove decisive in distinguishing between the author and his comrades.

The original diary began on page 25 and ended on page 147. On page 103, the clue I had been waiting for presented itself! The diarist casually mentioned the pay he received for a specific period of time.

> 26 September ... We only worked until 3:45 p.m. on account of pay which we received up to the end of June. I received $44.70... .

Now this was a statement that could be directly related to a specific individual on the company paylist! A check of No. 3 Company paylist for June failed to reveal any private soldier who received that sum. Again on page 112 the diarist mentioned his pay:

> **26 October** ... We received three months pay this afternoon
> viz. July, Aug. & Sept. I received $83.30... .

Once more I was unable to relate this lump sum payment to anything found in the paylists. However, his next entry concerning pay proved more helpful:

> **11 November** ... Pay for October $32.60.

Checking the paylist for October 1898 I found that under the "Cash Received" column three private soldiers had received $32.60! These men were: Private L. Lefevbre, E. Lincoln and H. Wakefield.[3] But now to distinguish our diarist from his two comrades?

Here is where my cumulative list of names mentioned by the author proved its worth. Our diarist had already referred to both Lefevbre and Wakefield as comrades in arms. I was fairly certain now that E. Lincoln was the diarist. To be absolutely certain, however, I once again sought the weight of evidence represented by a series of additional facts.

By the time I reached page 130 of the 147 page diary, I began to have a sinking feeling that my diligent search might yield only one slim proof of identity. Then on pages 132 and 134 the additional facts I needed suddenly materialized:

> **26 January** [1899] ... "Pay for Dec. $30.80... .

> **21 February** .... "Pay for January $21.55... .

I fumbled nervously with the dry dusty pages of the paylists, where the faded handwriting indicated that only one private soldier in No.3 Company received $30.80 - E. Lincoln. Similarly, the January paylist disclosed that only Pte. E. Lincoln, of all the enlisted men, received $21.55. There could be no doubt that Lincoln was "the unknown member of the Yukon Field Force" who, inadvertently or otherwise, had left his diary as a time capsule secreted amid the ruins of Fort Selkirk... .

With Lester's (alias Lincoln) identity firmly established, it only remained to confirm how the diary came into the possession of the late Miss Taylor. As I indicated earlier, the envelope, which contained the diary, bore the notation "Yukon Field Force Diary found in the old barracks at Fort Selkirk by Florence Taylor (probably in 1919)". The reference to the date of discovery was so vague, however, that I doubted whether the notation had actually been written by Miss Taylor. Perhaps it had been the work of a lawyer sent to inventory the estate after her death. In any case, I wanted to confirm the circumstances of the diary's discovery and if possible learn something of the life of the discoverer herself. Who was Miss Taylor and what had she been doing in the Yukon?

A copy of Florence Taylor's will had been forwarded by the executors along with the diary. The other beneficiaries, besides the Public Archives of Canada, included two brothers, one of whom, Mr. Charles Taylor, was still a resident of Whitehorse, in the Yukon Territory. While I was contemplating contacting him, a letter arrived from the Yukon Archives requesting a copy of the diary. Mr. Taylor had been informed of his sister's bequest to the Public Archives and told the local archivist of it. Within a short time the territorial archives had its copy of the diary and I had a transcript of an interview with Charlie Taylor concerning his late sister.

Florence Annie Taylor was born in Whitehorse, Yukon Territory on 8 August 1904, the daughter of Mr. and Mrs. Isaac Taylor. Mr. Taylor and William S. Drury were partners in the general merchandise firm of Taylor and Drury. The eldest child in the family, Florence received an excellent education which may account for her careful guardianship of the diary and its eventual donation to the Public Archives. After obtaining her primary and secondary education in local schools she was sent overseas at age 16 to attend the Clairemont School for Girls at Esher, England. Later schooling took place at the Sorbonne and the London School of Economics.

According to her brother, it was on a visit with her family about 1925, while staying with an uncle who managed the family store at Fort Selkirk, that she discovered the diary in the nearby abandoned barracks.

From about 1928 to 1932, Florence Taylor worked as assistant staff superintendent and later as a department manager for the

Woodwards Ltd. department store in Vancouver. In 1933, she emigrated to England and worked in the Juvenile Employment Office for the London Region until her retirement in 1969. She died in England on 28 May 1980, never knowing who the author of the diary was, or anything of his circumstances other than those revealed in the text of it.

END NOTES

1. Extracts from "Archival Detective Work: The Case of the Yukon Field Force Diary, in *Archivaria* 17 (Winter 1983-84) reproduced by permission of the editor.
2. Public Archives of Canada, Department of Militia and Defence, Record Group 9 II F 7 Volume 11.
3. PAC, Record Group 9 II F 7 Volume 12

EDWARD LESTER'S DIARY
"PLENTY OF GOOD HARD GRAFT"

[Material in square brackets and some punctuation has been added. The original diary is to be found in the Public Archives of Canada Manuscript Group 29, E 105.]

[Thursday May 19th, 1898]

... canvas sign displayed, with the following inscription "Stop: 3 tons of Freight and 5 Passengers". We now pass parallel to the glacier mentioned above and can see the edge which looks like an enormous ice cliff, displaying huge vertical gaps and fissures as if rent by an earthquake.* We still keep passing camps of stranded miners,** on two of which they displayed a Canadian Ensign and cheered us lustily; of course we returned the compliment with interest also with musical honours i.e. with a bugle obligato.

8.0 p.m. The current is now exceedingly swift owing to a freshet and is full of snag and tree trunks. In trying to avoid one of these floating logs, our pilot allowed the boat to swing broadside on and, the current catching her, dashed her into a pile of trees and driftwood, leaving a hole in her side 15 x 5 feet and below the water line. Of course the water rushed in and had we not had built-in compartments we must have sunk. One compartment was, however, filled, and much difficulty was found in plugging the hole. After this had been done the water was pumped out and we proceeded on our way.

An amusing incident occurred just after this. A crooked branch was lying across a log in the river; one end of it was in the water and the current caused it to bob up and down making

---

* "Here now is the great Orlebar or Great glacier, which measures five kilometers in length [? width] along the river and which reaches such an immense depth that one is unable to determine exactly where it ends. Facing it, on the other side of the river, are hot springs." Loicq du Lobel, *Le Klondyke, L'Alaska le Yukon et les iles Aleoutiennes*, (Paris, 1899), p. 9 [Translation libre]. See also Faith Fenton's description.

** "From time to time one sees a tent; those of poor miners going there [Glenora] over the ice, caught by the break-up and unable to get any further." —*ibid.*, p. 8.]

Chilkoot Pass 1067m
White Pass 889m
Dyea
Skagway
Tagish Lake
Atlin Lake
Teslin Lake
1967m
YUKON TERRITORY
BRITISH COLUMBIA
Swift River
MT. SNOWDEN 2130m
Disputed Boundary
COAST
CANADA U.S.A.
HAYES PEAK 1925m
Camp Victoria
Jennings River
Teslin
1955m
LYNN CANAL
N
Taku River
Disella L.
METAN MTN. 1819m
1955m
1937m
1969m
Inklin R.
Nahlin R.
Juneau
HEART PEAKS 2012m
Sheslay River
MESZAH PEAK 2164m
Stephens Passage
Admiralty Island
Hudson's Bay Post
1974m
Tuya R.
Tahltan R.
1660m
Telegraph Creek
Glenora
Chutine R.
Grand Canyon of the Stikine
1959m
Klootchman Canyon
MT. GORDON
BRITISH COLUMBIA
ALASKA
AMBITION MTN. 2938m
Mess Creek
FREDERICK SOUND
Kupreanof Island
MOUNTAINS
Stikine River
Grand Glacier
Iskut River
Wrangell

WRANGELL
TO TESLIN LAKE

| 0 | 20 | 40 | 60 | 80 | 100 km |
| 0 | 10 | 20 | 30 | 40 | 50 | 60 mi |

Ship •••••   Boat ➤   March ➡

it appear, in the fast fading light, just like a huge reptile half out of the water. So real did it appear that someone actually procured a rifle and fired twice at it before he discovered his mistake, which he did by the roars of laughter which followed his second shot.

Friday May 20th

Started at 4.0 a.m. At 6.0 a.m. met the *Ogilvie* on her return trip, she having started 24 hours before us, so she must have made a pretty quick passage. Morning fine and the sun shining brightly. We expect to reach Glenora sometime this afternoon.

11.30. We have just passed through a canyon so narrow that two of these steamers could scarcely lie abreast, the rocky sides rising hundreds of feet above us with a boiling current rushing between. The people on the boats quite expected to have to haul through, for the steam windlass was cleared and every preparation made, but with 100 lb. of steam air we slowly forged ahead and just managed to push through.

Whilst in the canyon, which, by the bye, is called the Klootchman's Canyon, we passed several parties working their way upstream in small boats. Of course it would be an utter impossibility to row a boat through against such current, so they had to tow; the men with the tow lines climbing like monkeys over the face of the rocky cliffs sometimes two or three hundred feet up, fighting their way literally foot by foot. We learned that only the day before one poor fellow, whilst engaged in this work, fell a distance of 150 ft. and was of course killed on the spot.

At 1.20 p.m., whilst at dinner, we were surprised to feel that the boat had stopped. It turned out that the boiler had become very foul and we had to put in to the bank whilst it was cleaned out. We stayed about an hour and a half and were allowed a run on shore. We all started looking for gold. One of the engineers got a shovelful of sand, washed it out in the shoals and the result was a few specks of gold. This is called "getting a colour".

At 5 p.m. we were in a part of the river where the current was ... .

[seven pages of the original manuscript are missing at this point

but M. Loicq du Lobel's narrative can fill in part of the story. This extract comes from p. 10 of his book].

"We traverse great rapids, through the Kloochman Canyon, then again more rapids. The water boils with power and fury, a river in turmoil. We advance 50 meters at a time with the aid of the capstan [hauling on a cable fixed to a tree or rock on shore].

"Once the captain orders full steam ahead and tries to advance without the help of the cable; but hardly is that order executed than we lose all the distance that we have gained with the capstan.

"Two boat loads of Indians pass with the speed of an arrow, going downstream.

"We inch laboriously upstream. The snow becomes less deep, the vegetation is more advanced, and now flowers become plentiful. In the interior spring comes earlier than on the coast; thus we arrive at Glenora and find masses of flowers in bloom, butterflies and many birds ... .

"At Glenora the whole town is on the beach, awaiting the arrival of the *Strathcona*, which brings the mail. Glenora is a town of tents which shelter a population of 2,500 men, most of whom came over the ice in the hope of reaching the Klondike by the Lake Teslin route.

"But there is no road and the poor men are stopped for want of money to pay their passages and transport their goods on a steamer going back downstream; and no one dares to descend the Stikine by boat or raft. Just for a moment these miners think that the troops are there to build a road but their hopes are soon dashed.*

"We establish our camp and go in search of horses and guides, but without any success. All the horses have been requisitioned for the soldiers who are going to clear a rough trail through the thick forests that must be traversed [to reach the

---

* "See miners resolutions wired [to] *Montreal Star* condemning Dominion Government for advertising Stikine route in Europe and now abandoning completion of promised wagon road. Feeling intense ... About five thousand miners stranded on route" — telegram from Glenora, H.J. Woodside to Clifford Sifton, 8 June 1898, copy in Woodside Papers, PAC, MG 30, C64, Vol. 23, file 4. Henry Joseph Woodside (1858 — 1933) entrepreneur, part-time soldier and turn-of-the-century photo-journalist, was *en route* to the Klondike himself. A committed Liberal, he would become editor of the *Yukon Sun*, 1898–1901.

Yukon].

"At Glenora the heat is overwhelming, the thermometer reaching 29 degrees Centigrade on the 24th of May* and 38 degrees Centigrade on the 25th. The nights are clear and one can read easily at 11 o'clock at night. The mosquitoes are terrible and our blood is poisoned [by their bites] so that our bodies are soon covered with small ulcers."

A sentry guarding stores at Glenora

[Loicq du Lobel and his family soon returned to Wrangell and took passage to Skagway. They went to Dyea by boat, crossed the Chilcoot Pass, and arrived at Dawson on 7 August 1898, while the bulk of the Yukon Field Force was still struggling over the trail to Teslin Lake. Lester's diary takes up the story again.]

* "Colonel Evans ordered a full dress parade for the morning of the Twenty-Fourth [Queen Victoria's birthday] and an afternoon of games and sports. The Force marched down from their campground above the tiny settlement to be greeted by several hundred Klondikers who had pitched camp around the small cluster of buildings within the last few days. The Colonel took the salute of his troops on the broad trail that served as the main street of the town. He ordered a *feu-de-joie* to be fired, and called upon the local Presbyterian minister to announce the exact hour of noon. The Rev. Mr. Pringle, perched on a wood pile, sextant in hand, called out the time as the sun crossed the meridian. Evans called for 'Three Cheers for the Queen' and again 'Three for the Klondike miners', then the crowd gave three and a tiger for 'The Colonel and the Yukon Force'. The sports events were a great success. The tug-of-war ended with a snapped rope. Someone opened a barrel of whiskey. A huge bearded miner in

Thursday June 2nd [at Glenora]

Beautiful day but terribly dusty owing to a brisk breeze.* The remainder of No. 1 Coy. left at 11 a.m. for Telegraph Creek with stores on board the *Elwood* under Capt Bennet. Company drill at 10 a.m. The *Elwood* brought mail. I got a St. John's *News* from Cotton but no letter. Spence however got one from him and in it he says he has not yet heard from me. This is very strange considering I sent him 2 post cards before leaving Vancouver.

It is marching order tomorrow — hope to goodness it won't be a repetition of yesterday as I have a blister on my heel caused by these damnable boots. Everyone is complaining of not getting enough to eat. Instead of double, we are not even getting full rations. All we had for supper tonight was two small buns about the size of a Boston cracker and a couple of spoonfuls of apples. There is something wrong somewhere.** Bob Langille seems very sick [and] he has been failing for some time.

At 12 (midnight) the Caledonia came in loaded with stores and No. 3 [Coy.] turned out for fatigue to unload her, which occupied us till 3 a.m.

Friday June 3rd

No marching order, or any other parade today for No. 3. No. 2 had a fatigue handling the freight which arrived in the night. Breakfast this morning was a very poor affair, a small piece of fat bacon, two small crackers and a couple of spoonfuls of fruit, not much for men who have been working all night.

---

sombrero and moccasins led the crowd in song. The Reverend Pringle set the woodpile alight, then despatched others to start bonfires on the hilltops. Evans ordered another salute to be fired. Another barrel was opened. As the column marched back to camp, the miners threw a few sticks of dynamite into the river as their salute." —A.L. Disher, "The Long March of the Yukon Field Force", in *The Beaver* (Autumn, 1962), pp. 9 and 10.

* From Glenora, Regimental-Sergeant-Major Young, RCD, wrote home to report that "We have been camped at Glenora about four days ... . This place is very sandy, the sand gets into everything we eat; mosquitoes and flies are not very bad considering it is ninety [degrees Fahrenheit] in the shade at midday." — *Winnipeg Daily Tribune*, 16 June 1898.

** Rations had been calculated at four lbs. per man per day, including beef, mutton, salt cod, bacon, bread, potatoes or fresh beans, rice, dried fruit, butter, salt, lard, sugar, and lime juice. — *Manitoba Morning Free Press*, 6 May 1898.

There were two races for prizes this evening, one for the single wheel cart [wheelbarrows] teams of 4 for [Nos.] 3 & 4 [companies] and one for [individuals] carrying a 50 lb. sack of flour. The team of No. 3 won the cart race. And a man from No. 1 Coy. won the other. Baker from No. 4 Depot was second.

Saturday June 4th

Rain this morning, but it cleared before parade. We had a march out but neither so hard or so far as before. [The] C[ommanding] O[fficer] seems to have taken a turnabout. We are getting better food, too, and are receiving a ration of fresh bread.

Rain again in the afternoon & evening. There was to have been a long distance race to Glenora & back with 45 lb. packs but the rain prevented it.

Rifle slings issued.

Sunday June 5th

It rained all night but cleared about Reveille. Church parade at 9.30 a.m.

Monday June 6th

Very hot with scorching sun. No drill parades, but we have been on the go all day with fatigues. I was issued with a pair of ankle boots, all hands received a ration of two plugs of tobacco, and we were issued with straps for carrying packs. They say we are to carry our large kit bags with all our belongings including our two double blankets & rubber sheet, the whole weighing 70 or 80 lbs.* I can hardly believe this; are we soldiers or pack mules? Nevertheless we are to parade with these packs tomorrow, without arms. This afternoon we put some provisions on board the *Strathcona* for the party at Telegraph Creek. This morning we shifted all the tents back a few yards.

---

* Current — 1980s — studies conclude that a fully fit soldier can carry up to one third of his body weight over extended distances outside combat. It is unlikely that the average YFF soldier weighed more than 80 kg.

Tuesday June 7th

We had the march out with the big kits today at 10 a.m. The sun was blazing although there was a little breeze. We marched to the flat above the old camp ground and back, about three miles in all. Four men from the left half-company fell out. On returning to camp they were made prisoners and got various terms of C[onfinement to] B[arracks] for using insubordinate language. L/Corp. Grey (Fredericton) refused to fall in at all, saying he was no d___d pack mule. He was made a prisoner, reduced [in rank to private] and discharged with ignominy.*

There have been several steamers in since yesterday & there is a rumour that some of us are to start tomorrow. There is an artilleryman returned from the advance party,** played out; I have not yet heard particulars.

It is impossible to get stamps for love or money. I have had a long letter written to Cotton, written & ready for the post this week or more, but am unable to procure the necessary stamps. Picquet tomorrow.

We had some more sports this evening.

Barrow Race, Officers vs Staff Sergts, won by latter.

Sack of Flour races won by Capt. Ogilvy & Pte. Flewelling.

Tug of War, Soldiers vs Civilians attached to the force. I was pulling in this. We won the first pull but they were too good for us in the next two pulls. N.B. I think we have seen the last of the big kits.

Wednesday June 8th

Immediately after reveille this morning (5.30) we got the order. Turn out No. 3 at once in marching order. The camp was immediately all bustle and on falling in we found our old friend the *Stikine Chief* alongside & No. 2 Coy. busy loading her up. We snatched a hasty breakfast as we were, in marching order, & after being served with a day's rations we struck tents &

---

* ["One of the companies ... said to be of Fredericton ... threatened to mutiny because they were being used as pack-mules and badly fed", reported the Ottawa *Evening Citizen*, 28 June 1898. "Commander Evans is having a lively time of it with his men."]
** A part of No. 1 Coy. had been sent out to reconnoitre the trail.

A river steamer comes alongside at Telegraph Creek

embarked at 9.0 a.m. en route for Telegraph Creek. We have on board No. 3 Coy., Capt. Ogilvy, Lt. Leduc & the Doctor, also Maj. Talbot & Capt. Gardiner: Before embarking Col. Evans paraded the left half-company separately & lectured them re the insubordination of yesterday, at the same time remitting the C.B. of the four offenders. I am detailed for guard on landing, so shall get out of the heavy fatigue which is certain to take place. Thank the Fates the day is fine or it would be miserable work pitching tents in the wet.

We got to Telegraph Creek at 2.0 p.m.* & started unloading

---

* In 1898 Glenora was the normal head of navigation on the Stikine, but at certain times, when water levels were just right, the river steamers could reach Telegraph Creek, 15

right away. We, on guard, have a snap watching the others work. Our guardroom was built out of boxes of biscuits & corned beef & roofed with tarpaulins. At 5.30 p.m. the boat was cleared & all the stores piled up in confusion on the wharf. I can plainly see plenty of good hard graft before we get through with it.

The "town" of Telegraph Creek has now about 350 inhabitants & was so named when there was a movement to connect this continent with the Old World by way of Alaska & Bering Straits (1866). The telegraph line had been laid over 900 miles when news came of the completion of the Atlantic cable & the work was abandoned.* At present the town contains two general stores, one hotel, two warehouses, a wharf in course of construction, two bakeries, one restaurant, & about a dozen log houses; the balance of the inhabitants live in tents. A large proportion of the people appear to be Indians. The guard stays with the stores: the camp is pitched about a mile & a half up the creek, the road up to it being very steep & rough.

Thursday June 9th

Last night we slept in the open air rolled in our blankets, having been strengthened by three more men & issued with loose ball ammunition with orders to shoot if necessary. We dismounted the guard at 9.30 a.m. and marched up to the camp by a very steep & rough waggon road.

The camp is picturesquely situated on two flats overlooking the creek on the opposite side to the road. No. 1 Coy. are on the first flat & Nos. 2 & 3 will be on the flat or terrace above, so that we can look down into No. 1 Coy.'s lines about 200 ft below us; the descent is so precipitous that the road from one terrace to the other has to be zig-zagged. The kitchens are at the bottom of the valley on the banks of the creek, of which the water is very clear & icy cold. Opposite the camp & by the roadside are the

---

kilometers upstream, at the foot of the Grand Canyon of the Stikine. Today, when Glenora is little more than a point on a map, communication is from the interior (via a dry-weather 350 km road that runs through Dease Lake to Watson Lake on the Alaska highway). Telegraph Creek boasts a radio station and airstrip. The old trail between Telegraph Creek and Glenora still exists but no scheduled boats ply the Stikine.

* See W.W. Bride and W.G. Crisp, "Telegraph Creek," in *The Beaver* (March, 1942), pp. 12-17, for a fuller story.

Q[uarter] M[aster's] Stores, & here the quarter-guard is mounted.

Both companies are on fatigue packing boxes & bales up from the wharf to the camp with the straps which were issued at Glenora & which, by the bye, are known as "tump lines". There was a fatigue from 6 to 8 p.m. Mailed letters to Cotton & home.

Friday June 10th

Reveille at 4 a.m. Breakfast at 4.45, fall in for fatigue at 5 a.m. Packing up the stores till 9.0 a.m. We are getting 4 meals a day & double working pay whilst we are getting the stores up. No work during the heat of the day. Started again at 6 p.m. & worked till 8 p.m. Supper at 8.30. I feel as fit as a fiddle & not a bit fagged.

There are a lot of Indians in this place. They belong to what is known as the "Siwash" Tribe & are not at all like the Indians of the Western Prairies. They say there is a Japanese strain in them which would account for the strong Mongolian cast of features seen in many of them.

The remainder of No. 1 Company start tomorrow with the Colonel for Teslin.

Saturday June 11th

Up at 4 a.m. again this morning & work from 5.30 to 9 a.m., dinner at 11.0. No work during the day except a few odd jobs about camp. Then tea at 5. Work from 6 to 8 & supper at 8.30. Made a new zigzag from the top terrace to the creek. The weather still continues tropical during the day, but turns cold at night. It is quite light at 10.15 p.m. & there is only semi-darkness from about 11.30 p.m. to 1.0 a.m.

The remainder of No. 1 Coy., with the Colonel, started this morning about 8 a.m. Three of the ladies accompanied them.

Issued with what is supposed to be a two month's supply of tobacco, but through a mistake of Sgt. Lapierre's our section only got 4 plugs. I got two extra plugs from Bobbie Graham which gives me, with what I already have, 7 1/2 plugs, so I suppose I shall rub along. The Colonel returned to camp this evening.

Sunday June 12th

Although today is Sunday it has been anything but a day of rest for us. Fatigues were going on all the time. There was Church parade at 7 a.m. Immediately after breakfast I was sent on fatigue down to a wharf to look for a certain box; we had to handle nearly all the freight & then did not find what we came for. We brought up however a lot of camp kettles, frying pans, etc.

The weather if anything is hotter than ever. The wild flowers here, specimens of which I have been sending home are in many case identical with the flowers of the Old Country. There are quantities of wild roses, but they are not the familiar pink & white of the English dog rose but are of a deep red colour. There are wild strawberries, gooseberries, raspberries, & currants. Thousands of butterflies flit about, the commonest being a large size and very like, if not identical with, the "Swallowtail" of England. Of animals I have seen very few up to now, though they say there are bear, deer & antelope to be had, also porcupines. Birds too, seem to be very scarce, though some ducks have been shot on a lake not far away.

I am for guard at 6 p.m. with Platt & Lowe. We dismount at 9 a.m. tomorrow & are known as the Quarter of Telegraph Creek Guard, to distinguish us from the guard at the wharf which is called the Stikine Guard & stays on 24 hours.

7 p.m. On guard so have a chance of writing a few lines in peace, that is if the mosquitoes which are out in force will allow me. I will describe as near as possible the position of the Camp. The valley of the creek winds upwards from the Stikine River between high bluffs & about 100 ft up, on the left looking up the valley, is the waggon road cut out of the side of the hill. On the right the ground rises in three enormous steps as it were, forming a series of plateau or terraces, & on these the camp is pitched.

The waggon road extends for five or six miles beyond the camp & was constructed by Messrs. Mackenzie & Mann. The work for some reason is now at a standstill * & consequently the

---

* The Yukon Railway Bill, which would have legalized the government's agreement with Mackenzie and Mann, had been procedurally thwarted in the Senate in April. It was blocked

remainder of the road to Teslin Lake is simply an Indian trail. This is reported to be in fairly good condition as far as the Tahltan River (25 to 30 miles). I hear it is pretty tough after. However, I suppose we shall get there somehow. There is, I believe, a party of ax-men to be selected from all Companies who are to set out at once & push right on to Teslin; they are to bridge & "corduroy" when necessary. I must knock off now as the mosquitoes are chewing lumps out of me.

Monday June 13th

As we have no facilities for sleeping on guard we built a fire & sat round all last night smoking & spinning yarns. Dismounted guard at 9 a.m. Usual work going on. Platt, Lowe & I slept out in the open, rolled in our blankets, & found it more comfortable than the crowded tent.

Tuesday June 14th

Fatigue as usual at 5.30 a.m. & 6 p.m. We have now got nearly all the stores up. The mail came in yesterday, I got a whole budget of papers. The ax party started this morning with Maj. Talbot & Sgt.Major Young.

Wednesday June 15th

Usual routine. The stores at the Stikine are now almost all packed up to camp & I don't think there will be any left after today. It has come over very cloudy since noon & looks like rain.

6 p.m. There was no fatigue tonight as all the freight is up except a few heavy packages.

Thursday June 16th

Raining this morning but we turned out at 5.30 p.m. & carried up one load, when the rain stopped further work so we had a morning off. It cleared up about noon & we turned out for fatigue in the evening. I don't think I mentioned the dust before,

---

in such a way that there was little prospect of it ever being taken up again. (See Senate Debates 1898 and Clifford Sifton to H.J. Woodside, 2 July 1898, in PAC, MG 30, C64, Vol. 23, file 4). The contractor, who had already started work in response to the administration's urging, promptly stopped and construction never resumed.

it is something awful. In a very little time after washing, we are as black as tinkers. Everything is the same, valises, harnesses, kit bags & all, filthy. We have given up washing more than twice a day & as most of us never shave except when for duty we are a nice looking crush.

I hear there is a big pack train to start tomorrow with an escort from No.2 Coy.

Friday June 17th

Fine day. Fatigue as usual at 5.30 a.m. but there is not much left to bring up, only made two trips & then Platt & I only carried two loads between us. Started raining at 7.0 p.m. Carried up the last load from the wharf this evening. Stikine Guard discontinued. The pack train started this morning with a Corporal & two men as escort.

Saturday June 18th

Fine but cloudy. Reveille at 5.0 as usual but no fatigue except just cleaning up camp. Yesterday Walker started on horseback for Glenora to fetch back the mail but has not yet returned. Doctor's Inspection at 2.0 p.m. At 3 p.m. Walker returned with the mail. I got some papers from home, forwarded by Cotton, but no letter either from home or St. Johns.

A mule train came through our lines this afternoon & just as one of the mules got opposite our tent, he started kicking, kicked his trace off, & head over heels he went, down the steep bank into the lines below, & a nice old time they had getting him up again. The beggar seemed to know just what they wanted him to do & then go and do exactly the opposite. Finally they had to lug him up with a mounted mule & a lariat.

We have had a holiday today: no work at all.

Sunday June 19th

It has been raining all night & is still raining. Church Parade altered from 7 to 10 a.m. & then postponed indefinitely. Yesterday the vacancies in our tent caused by the men who have gone away with the ax party, were filled , Corp. Hansen taking Corp. Hanlon's place. There are now in our tent Sgt. Lapierre, Corp.

Hansen, Fowler, Platt, myself, Spence, Lefevbre, Doré, Graham, Hayes, McGowan & Lowe.

There is a report going the rounds that forty Indians have "gone wild" up the trail & have killed one man & wounded

A sentry at Telegraph Creek is admonished for some neglect of duty

another. I think, however, it is merely a yarn. The Doctor was sent for this afternoon for someone on one of the advance parties, I have not heard who it is. It has been raining all day and is still at it.

(Retreat). We have not been out of the tent all day. Our tent is, however, fairly waterproof so we are pretty comfortable & thanks to the two batches of papers received last week are well provided with reading matter. I am reading just now *An Ocean Tragedy* by Clark Russell. Our kits & rifles are all piled outside the tents covered as far as possible with rubber sheets, but I expect they will be in a pretty state after all this rain.

At 8.30 mail came in & I got another batch of papers but still no letters.

Monday June 20th

No rain this morning but very dull & cloudy. No fatigue but just cleaning up around camp, so we improved the shining hour by cleaning up our arms & accoutrements & a nice job it was, but as last we succeeded in restoring them to their normal condition.

The sick man ahead is said to be G[unne]r Dumais, who is said to be suffering from Mountain fever & is very bad. The medical arrangements here are simply abominable. McGowan was sick this morning & was seen by one of the nurses in the absence of the Doctor.* This did not do much good as the Dr. had gone off with keys of the medicine pannier & nothing in the way of medicine was to be had but a few cathartic pills. This is not as it should be — there is no Dr., no hospital sergeant & no orderly in camp.

It is said that the last party who started from here have run short of provisions & two men, Baker & Lefebvre, were sent with sufficient to last them till tomorrow. They are 5 miles up the trail & consist of Corp. Blake-Forster & party who started on the [illegible].

The Dr. returned about Retreat.

Tuesday June 21st

Reveille at 6 a.m. & breakfast at 7.30. Twenty men of our Coy. & all available from No. 2 started for Blake-Forster's camp this morning. I am for guard tonight, so did not go. They took a days' ration with them, so will be away all day.

Yesterday a young fellow, a civilian whom we all know by sight, was killed or drowned in the Stikine. He was on the opposite side of the river prospecting & was struck on the back by a falling rock & pushed into the river. He rose once only & was

---

* "The Nurses of the Victorian Order proved of great service to the Force, scattered as it was for several months over a distance of nearly six hundred miles. The Nurses were divided into two parties and sent with separate detachments and, with the Surgeon Major and Hospital Sergeant, formed a chain which enabled all portions of the Force to be within touch, should illness or accident occur, with trained assistance. The appreciation of all ranks of the Force took tangible form in a contribution of three hundred and fifty dollars towards the cost of the cabin at present being built by the Victorian Nurses at Dawson." — Evans to Adjutant-General, Ottawa, 1 November 1898, in D Hist 73/78

never seen after. There was also a sudden death at Telegraph [Creek] last night.

All news as to the condition of the trail & of the progress of the advance party is utterly unreliable. There is a report that the ax party with the Sgt.-Major has passed the others & is making 20 miles a day; how true this may be it is impossible to say; I for one do not believe it.

Mounted guard at 6 p.m. with Platt & Hayes; Corp. Shaw [was] commander.

Wednesday June 22nd

Fine morning. Dismounted guard at 9 a.m. Flying sentry mounts during the day. Large pack train left with one of the nurses & one man.

Thursday June 23rd

Pouring wet morning - nothing to do but to lie off & read write & smoke. We are all complete in the tent but Spence who is on guard. I am engaged on a letter home so as to have it ready for the next mail. Cleared up towards noon. Started reading *The Iron Pirate* by Max Pemberton.

Friday June 24th

Fine morning. Orderly man. No further movement of the troops. Finished letter home giving details of journey from Ottawa to Wrangle [sic.]. Platt & I ascended the hill overlooking the camp this evening; we took a rough sketch of the camp which I am sending home, together with some pressed flowers.

Saturday June 25th

Drs. Inspection at 2 p.m. Wrote to Cotton.

10 p.m. The sun is still shining on the mountain tops although set to us. There was a mail in this evening & Platt got a letter direct from England & not via St. John's, but there was nothing for me. I was very disappointed & think it more than enough not to have heard for so long.

There has been nothing fresh all day & I am beginning to

weary of the monotony & shall be glad when we make a move.*

A turn-of-the-century Tahltan shaman surrounded by dancers at Telegraph Creek.

Sunday June 26th

Beautiful morning. Church parade for Catholics at 7.30 a.m. Service in camp. The Church of England contingent had to march to Telegraph Creek. Mailed letters to Cotton & my mother. The mosquitoes are a holy terror tonight & we have to keep up a small 'smudge' (smokey fire) in front of each tent to prevent ourselves being eaten up alive. Occasionally we have to make a small one inside the tent itself to drive the devils out.

* The delay was caused by a shortage of pack animals. "The Hudson's Bay Company claim not to have had sufficient time between acceptance of the contract and arrival of the troops at Glenora to complete its arrangements ... it was apparent that the Company had, at first, failed to grasp the magnitude of the work to be performed, and had not provided the necessary number of pack animals." — Evans to Adjutant-General, 1 November 1898, in D Hist 73/78. In fact the HBC had provided only 141 pack animals, while at least 300 were required to move the Force's eighty tons of supplies up the trail in one lift. Major Bliss had to badger the HBC for a week to gather another 170 horses and mules, dickering with owners against the many parties of private citizens also trying to hire animals. — See Georgina Foster letter in the Toronto *Globe*, 15 October 1898. M. Loicq du Lobel, it will be recalled, abandoned the attempt to hire transport when he found that Bliss had cornered the supply.

Monday June 27th

Started raining during the night & continued till 9 o'clock this morning. There were 12 of us warned for fatigue this morning. We marched up to Blake-Forster's camp where most of the stores now are. Here we did some packing up & after having lunch marched back to camp arriving about 2.30 p.m. Corp. Blake-Forster & his men, now six in number, seem to be having a fine time of it.

Tuesday June 28th

Fine morning. Maj. Young with Kelly & Wesley started out this morning. The Major was mounted. Capt. Gardiner in charge of camp. Fatigue party from left half-coy. for Blake-Forster's.

Wednesday June 29th

Glorious day. Nothing worthy of note occurred all day. I must, however, record our supper tonight: it consisted of hash, stewed prunes, boiled rice, cakes & butter, also about a pint of delicious strawberries gathered by Jack Platt this afternoon. Read *The Beautiful White Devil* by Guy Boothly: Verdict, well worth reading. Tonight some of the boys chased & killed a small porcupine. It was only a young one, the quills being only 3 ins in length.

Thursday June 30th

Another fine day. All hands in our tent turned out to gather pine tops for the tent floor. This makes a very sweet carpet & saves a lot of dirt. Read a book called *Lewy & I* which I thought rather stupid.

Friday July 1st

Still keeps fine with a hot sun but there is a cool breeze blowing today. Waiting guard tonight, so shall be flying sentry tomorrow. They say there is a big batch of mail at Glenora. Rev. Mr. Pringle* came into camp today & brought us some stamps.

---

* The Reverend Dr. John Pringle, born in Charlottetown, PEI, in 1852, was a Presbyterian divine of the 'muscular christian' variety. Six feet two and well-built, "he had established a

The ax party are said to be at Teslin Lake & the other party close up. Major Young returned to camp today but without Wesley & Kelly.

Saturday July 2nd

Fine & warm. Flying sentry on QM stores.* It is a pretty easy job but rather lonesome. No mail to hand yet.

Sunday July 3rd

Cloudy & a little rain. Usual Church parades. Captain Thacker started for Glenora for mail early this morning. Through some mistake on the C. of E. parade, Capt. Ogilvy has ordered a drill parade tomorrow. Mail came in this evening & I received the M[an]c[hester] papers & a *Regiment*. The latter paper was for June 2nd, addressed direct, so they must have had my letter from Vancouver, but I got no letter from anyone at home which is to say the least of it very strange.

Monday July 4th

Fine morning.

10 a.m. Squad drill in 'clean fatigue' dress. This drill was a punishment drill ordered by Capt. Ogilvy & lasted till 12 o'clock. We are to get it till we are "Smartened up". The same gallant officer has ordered a kit inspection for No. 3 Coy. at 2 o'clock tomorrow.

We have been here since the 18th of June & have been drinking the creek water which I may here say is perfectly good & sweet, cold & clear as crystal. Today the Dr. has discovered it to be impure & all have been forbidden to drink it. A fatigue has been detailed to carry up water daily from a so-called spring about 3/4 of a mile down the trail. I make no comments.

---

record for the longest tramp in a day carrying the largest pack, 400 pounds. He wore moccasins and sprang off his toes like an Indian" ("Rachel Hanna's Diary," in the *Bracebridge Herald-Gazette*, 11 April 1974). He subsequently served in the Yukon — where he was joined by his younger brother, the Reverend George — until 1907 when he took a parish at Sydney, N.S. He joined the Canadian Expeditionary Force in 1915 and was Mentioned in Despatches during the one month he spent in the line with the 1st Infantry Brigade. But, at 63, he was too old for the rigours of the trenches and he spent most of the war as a chaplain at Base Hospitals.

*A flying sentry had a fixed duty but was free to move at will through the area to be guarded.

Today being 'Independence Day', the 'Stars & Stripes' is much in evidence at Telegraph Creek & they have been banging away with rifles & revolvers all day. There are some sports tonight to which most of the boys are going but I think I shall stay in camp & read the papers I got yesterday.

Tuesday July 5th

I altered my mind last night & went down to the sports after all. Our boys did not do badly; Wakefield won the high jump with 4 ft 9 ins & the long jump with 16 ft. Flewelling was 2nd in the 200 yds & the Military won the Tug of War. The sports were followed by a dance to which I did not go.

There was kit inspection at 2 p.m.

Wednesday July 6th

A few men went on fatigue up to Blake-Forster's camp which, by the way, is called Camp Wolseley. They report nearly all the stores gone & as there is only a small quantity left here I am in hopes we shall be making a move soon. Only the 'marked men' were for drill today.

Thursday July 7th

Another glorious day. Water fatigue at 8 a.m. Squad drill at 10 a.m., for No. 3 only of course. We had another example of Capt. O's peculiarities last night when he changed all the NCOs in charge of the tents, putting the r[igh]t. half-company Non-Commissioned [Officers] with the left half-company & vice versa - what for, God only knows, but I know he is exasperating the company very much.

Friday July 8th

Broiling hot day. Squad drill at 10 a.m. for No. 3. Most of us were dismissed but some fourteen or fifteen names were taken for extra drill. The general dissatisfaction which has been brewing nearly came to a crisis last night and almost resulted in serious consequences when orders came out: they called for kit inspections for both Companies. Now considering that No. 3 only showed kit last Tuesday, & all showed a good kit, it was

The Yukon Field Force at Telegraph Creek June, 1898

certainly out of all reason to order them to show again. The whole of No. 3 Company were therefore unanimously resolved not to show. Their intention was to leave camp en masse about 9 a.m. & not to return till after the inspection was over. Luckily Maj. Young, who was out of camp when orders were promulgated, returned & issued an after [sic] order that No. 3 would not show & so a catastrophe was avoided, as of course the action of the company would have been rank mutiny.

In the evening Platt, McGill & I climbed the hill above the camp but soon returned on account of the mosquitoes.

Saturday July 9th

Another blazing hot day. No. 2 showed kit at 2 p.m. Hayes & I went down to Telegraph [Creek] with Colour-Sgt. Campbell to bring up some salmon but could not get any. We returned, however, in the evening & procured 52 lbs caught by an Indian in a seine net some 3/4 miles down the river. Orders for No. 3 Coy to march on Monday at 6 a.m.

Sunday July 10th

Church 9.30 a.m. Busy all morning packing kit bags & washing our clothes. How some of my old friends would have laughed to have seen me with my sleeves rolled up doing my own laundry. We are allowed two large kit bags between two men. The blankets (two per man with rubber sheets) go in one & our spare kit in the other. Platt & I are together.

Dinner today was a regular 'skin tightener'. The following menu was posted at No. 3 Coy.'s kitchen.

"Farewell Dinner

Pea Soup

Fried Salmon

Boiled Spuds

Hard Tack

Extra

Bully Beef"

FAITH FENTON'S DESPATCHES
SPECIAL CORRESPONDENCE OF THE GLOBE

Faith Fenton had joined the Field Force at Vancouver and her reports of the journey north, which provide something of a contrast to Lester's account, appeared in the Toronto Globe *between 4 June and 30 October. The first of them follows. Fenton tended to gush a good deal over sunrises, sunsets, scenery and "our gallant boys"; to avoid boring the modern reader, some material of that kind has been excised.*

Wrangel, May 16 1898 ...The little knot of men on the wharf, with their lanterns gleaming in the pale morning light, hurrahed with a will as our vessel moved slowly out into the harbour. Vancouver lay sleeping under an opal sky. The velvet-misted mountains stood in clear cut relief against their translucent background... .

The first engagement of the Yukon Field Force began before the *Islander* was fairly under way when, on proceeding to go aboard, our troops found 60 or more civilian Klondikers from various parts already in possession of staterooms and berths. There was a battle royal upon the wharf, the combattants being officers of the Yukon Field Force and the C.P.R. Company. The result was victory for the former, who calmly took possession, while the unfortunate civilians who had secured and paid for comfortable passage at Victoria were compelled to bunk out in the byeways and hedges of the vessel. But since the situation was evidently neither the fault of the Force nor the civilians, as much courtesy as possible was shown in the matter and Sunday morning - the first on board - found the entire ship's company shaken down, if not into comfort, at least into a peaceable discomfort, the weather helping out by being gloriously fine during the entire three days trip.

It may be interesting, just at this point, for the many *Globe* readers who desire to follow the adventures of the expedition, to know the full personnel of the Force according to the Colonel's notebook. Two hundred and one military, twelve officers inclusive, * nine artificers (boat builders, packers, etc.), nine civilians (Civil Service staff, Department of the Interior), six women (four Victorian Order nursing staff, and one little lady who goes to her husband, an officer in the Mounted Police at Dawson), and last but not least, the regimental dogs - "Spud", the Colonel's Irish terrier; Capt. Burstall's water spaniel, and "Jeff", a collie of doubtful ancestry who attached himself at Vancouver, and in whom the men take a special interest as the 'yaller dog' of the party. Not to be forgotten, either, are the sixty horses, who are in the clover of laziness now, but whose work will begin at Glenora... .

The inside channel trip from Vancouver to Wrangel is very beautiful, not unlike the far-famed Saguenay River in somber scenery, not unlike the Georgian Bay inside channel in route, yet surpassing both these as snow-covered mountains and deep-sea waters dwarf all lesser grandeur... .

...A ship's company usually manages to have a jolly time when they are thrown together for even a few days, and in the exceptional circumstances of a force of redcoats being aboard the fun is apt to be unflagging. The spirits of the sturdy young fellows must 'have a vent' and 'our boys' found it in morning athletics and evening entertainments of various sorts. The concerts are always popular and the Force did their best, being ably assisted by many of the civilian Klondikers.

A Klondike boat gathers a curious variety of passengers — men from all parts of the world who have seen strange things and passed through unique experiences. The first night aboard Surgeon-Major Foster was called to prescribe for a sick fellow, a miner from South Africa, who was suffering from malaria and had taken several 'chill spells'. The doctor administered quinine and left him. When he went to look for him in the morning, the man had disappeared, and search failed to find him for a day and a night. Just as everyone concluded that he had gone overboard,

---

* There were certainly twelve officers with the Force. But according to the May 1-14, 1898, paylist preserved in the Public Archives (RG 9, II, F 7, Vol. 11)there were only 184 other ranks on strength, giving a total of 196 military personnel in the party. The *Report of the Department of Militia and Defence* for 1898 says the Force consisted of 15 NCO's and men from the Royal Canadian Dragoons, 16 from the Royal Canadian Artillery's Field Division

he emerged from some corner, pale, but evidently better for the season.

Two dining room waiters, newly engaged for the trip, are discovered to possess guitars. They are seized upon and induced to play for "Black Billy", the potato peeler, who is all abeam at the prospect of giving a "hoe down befoah de Cuh'nel an' ladies". As they sweep the strings we recognize the professional touch; they play on mouth organs, jews' harps; they sing with dramatic expression and effect; they are, in fact, as we afterwards discover, expert stage variety men, working their way to the Klondike.

A French count [M. Loicq du Lobel] with his party - wife, daughters and sons - has come all the way from Paris to discover whether there really is such a place as Klondike, that gay city being rather sceptical in this matter, as it is about most things. He is delighted with the Yukon Field Force and meditates following all the way to Fort Selkirk as a vanguard [sic] and perhaps "enveest une leetle."

Mining engineers, who know the world as a very little place; surveyors, moneyed speculators, traders, working miners with just enough to carry them through; and men of shady dress and shadier faces, weave a medley passenger list on any vessel bound for the Klondike. Yet the touch of nature that proclaims human kinship is present in them all. They are hungry, weary, sick or buoyant; they are full of eagerness, hope or despondency. They dare harsh things and evil actions; yet a simple home melody draws the roughest and most cynical from the far deck corner within hearing of the knot gathered about the singer. And when the night drops upon the vessel, making its steady, throbbing way up between Alaskan mountain heights, the tramp Klondiker rolled in his blanket down among the horses sleeps as deeply, as restfully and safely, as does the Colonel in his stateroom.

Wrangel [sic] is indescribable to anyone who has never seen a boom town. Coming into dock, when the tide is low, it looks to be chiefly wharfage propped on a thousand legs. At high tide the

and 30 from its Garrison Division, and 130 from the Royal Regiment of Canadian Infantry; giving a total of 191 other ranks and 203 altogether.

legs are less in evidence, and we have a chance to discover that there are houses and tents in almost equal number. Everything is new in Wrangel. The chief hotel — a really good establishment for the place — is two months old; the majority of shops are four weeks old; while the residences, tents and shacks, can be reckoned by weeks. The population floats pretty much with the tide, fluctuating up and down the coast according to the latest reports of [gold] "finds". Sometimes an outgoing boat will deplete the town considerably, but an incoming vessel is likely to supply the deficit with new residents.

The queer little place is rather quiet just now, so the oldest inhabitant asserts. But when the 'clean up' comes down, a great rush is expected. Land speculators at Wrangel were sadly put out at the non-passage of the Yukon Railway bill. They bought largely and paid high prices in anticipation. February and March found them very blue; but now that British Columbia has taken up the project their hopes have revived.*

Architecturally, Wrangel suggests a series of Quebec's lower town alleys reproduced in wood and canvas. There are no streets — each building, shack or tent, has squatted at will and everybody strolls through everybody else's backyard. The population is just as much of a pepperpot sprinkle. The lady doctor from Los Angeles, with professional bag in hand, steps blithely out of her tent quarters to visit a patient in a six-bunked, single-roomed shanty across the way. Two young lawyers are having a game of poker on a soap-box inside the doorway of their 'office'. Correspondents and artists representing some of the world's biggest journals stroll about in roughing suits, awaiting vessels and picking up points. Klondikers in the regulation yellow knee boots and sombrero are everywhere and the smell of pine boards and the sound of the hammer and plane is over it all.

Wrangel is rich in spicy mining stories and incidents, if only

---

* On 10 June 1898 the *Globe* reported that the British Columbia government had voted Mackenzie and Mann, the thwarted railway constructors, a $4,000 per mile cash subsidy "for the construction of an all-Canadian line from Teslin Lake to a British seaport" — actually to Port Simpson, immediately south of the tip of the Alaskan 'panhandle'. "When this amount was voted by the Local House, it was confidently expected that the Dominion Government, without a question of a doubt, would to a greater or less extent supplement this subsidy either by a money or land grant...[but] this appears not to be the case, and consequently the construction of the road will in all probability not go on."

we had time to collect them. But our stay is limited to a few hours. Already we are transferred on board our river boats, *Strathcona* and *Stikine Chief*, and with the rising of the tide the Yukon Field Force begins its five days' trip up the Stikine to Glenora, where a longer delay will give chance for a fuller chat.

Glenora, May 27. When a traveller arrives this far on his journey to the Klondike, he begins to understand the conflict of report that travels eastward. It is not that all men are liars up in this country — that is, to any greater extent than they are at large — but that the conditions are continually changing, and in the present season of the year the changes occur with greater rapidity then our present slow system of communication with the outside world can record. If it were possible to overtake copy on its journey eastward, much of it would be 'killed' by the correspondent who, at the time of writing, was expressing the exact truth.

Take the Stikine River, for example. A little more than a month ago it was covered with ice, and dog-sleds were toiling over its surface. For the past two weeks, ten or twelve steamers have been plying up and down with careful soundings of its shallow waters. Today, every boat is tied up somewhere along the banks, and passengers and crews are making the best of the situation — a swollen river with a current against which it is impossible to make headway — and the tie-up may last for a week. Campers along the shore are being inundated and are hastily moving to higher ground.

...If Stikine River weather and water are uncertain, Stikine time is even more so. There appears to be no standard of regulation after a vessel leaves Vancouver. Every man's watch is a law unto itself. There is 'Wrangel time' and 'steamboat time', 'mountain time' and 'Glenora time', the variations lying anywhere between five minutes and twenty times five. The wise traveller in these regions is willing to trust his watch alone, for presently, like Bo Peep's sheep, the stray minutes come trooping back and adjust themselves to his particular record.

The event of Queen's Birthday in Glenora, after that chiefest one of firing a *feu de joie* and cheering her Most Gracious

Majesty, was the announcement made by the Rev. Mr. Pringle, from the top of a woodpile and with watch in hand, that by sextant observation just taken, the sun declared itself exactly in meridian and all of Her Majesty's Glenora subjects might set their timepieces at the hour of noon.

That was a pretty moment in the life of this little far northern village of tents. The entire [Yukon Field] force had marched down from the campground and flashed its scarlet ranks along the broad trail that stands for the one Glenora street. The men made a splendid appearance, and none would have guessed the hard work of pitching tents and storing supplies that had been undergone the day before. The march past and the salute, cheers for the Queen and again for the Klondike miners, with a responsive cheer from the miners for Colonel Evans and the Yukon force, this was the movement and sound, but only an artist could have caught the vivid coloring. Ranks of red coats outlined against white canvas tents and piney shacks, and flanked on either side by several hundred civilians — all sorts and conditions of men in all sorts of attire. Sombreros, knee-high moccasins, sweaters, men unshaved and collarless but splendid in bronzed strength; beyond these again, pack animals browsing, slow-moving oxen, and mules whose heels gave startled emphasis to the rattle of musketry; in the background, the ever-present hills, and in from the narrow, swift-rushing river... .

In the afternoon there were sports, various races, and a tug-of-war that only ended when the much-tried rope gave way with a snap, precipitating the sturdy contestants into inglorious heaps. In the evening bonfires lit the hilltops, while a huge, heart-warming fellow roared and crackled its flame accompaniment to our camp concert.

So Glenora, the little village of tents in the Queen's far north, celebrated her lady's birthday.

Glenora, June 1 - A trip up the Stikine might be a trip down the St. Lawrence as far as comfort is concerned. These new river boats — and it is asserted that thirty of them have been built for this special route during the past season — are quite as well appointed as those in the east. We have electric light, table napkins, fresh fruit for breakfast. Possibly we might have finger bowls also, if we asked for them.*It strikes one as a novel and unexpected thing that away up the shallow, snaggy river, in the heart of the northern Rockies, where a year ago nothing beyond an occasional raft passed up [sic] and down, such comforts of civilisation should now prevail. Civilisation follows trade, and trade follows the gold rush at a feverish pace, pitiful in its revelation... .

It was a relief to us all when we left Wrangel, with its odor of unsanctity, material and spiritual. To lovers of civic order and wholesomeness, Wrangel is offensive. We remember it as a blot. We realise with pride that such a town would be impossible in Canada. The United States has yet to learn how to govern annexed territory.

Yet it held for us one redeeming feature, due to the present cordial national *entente*. A Wrangel audience sang "God Save The Queen" in its theatre one evening last week, and Wrangel celebrated the Queen's Birthday as heartily as it will the coming 4th of July. There is some good stuff remaining in this wide, open, lawless little town after all.

The passing of the Yukon Field Force has been of excellent effect thus far in both Canadian and American territory. It is good for Canada's western prairie towns and coast cities, where no infantry schools yet exist, to see what a fine body of regulars can be gathered at instant call for service in any part of the Dominion - not foreigners, not even Imperial troops, but Canadian boys, trained in Canadian service. It stimulates civic pride and strengthens confidence in Canada's ability to look after her own.

Upon the Americans the effect is even more marked. At Wrangel the entire town— a miscellaneous and dubious assortment of nationalities —assembled upon the dock to survey the Canadian redcoats as the *Islander* swung into her moorings. Correspondents of big American dailies were busy with pad and pencil; river and coastal boats carried word up the Alaskan

---

* It should be borne in mind that Fenton, the nurses, Mrs. Starnes and the officers of the Field Force were travelling first-class; the other ranks — Lester and his peers — were not

coast and into the heart of the mining district, that so prompt is Canada in action, so insistent upon the preservation of order and good government in its most outlying territories, that a body of troops are already entering the Yukon gold regions to establish a base of support, if required, for the splendid work of the Mounted Police ... .

The effects reach wider yet. In Australia, South Africa, the British Isles, and on the continent [of Europe] men to whom the Klondike is yet but a word to conjure with will read, digest, and govern their dispositions in emigration accordingly. Apart from any direct return of service, such indirect results alone are worth the cost of the expedition to the Canadian people and Government.

The Stikine River is the most shallow, snaggy and uncertain body of water in our somewhat extensive acquaintance with Canadian rivers. It curves and doubles; it is full of sandbars; it has a tremendous current, and is the muddiest river in the country. Like most mountain rivers, it varies continually in depth, according to the season of the year and the weather. If the latter be warm, the melting snow on these splendid mountain heights pours down in cascades and fissure-rivulets — pretty water babies that gleam in the sunlight and play and leap down the grim boulders. If the weather be cool, the river falls rapidly, dropping sometimes as much as six feet in a night. A boat that ties up to the bank for the night occasionally finds itself stranded in the morning. As it is only very recently that the river has come to be a transportation route, pilots acquainted with its vagaries are few; consequently, since its opening to navigation some two weeks ago, the numerous new river boats are running go-as-you-please trips, both in time and route.

At Wrangel we are told that the trip up the river to Glenora — a distance of one hundred and fifty miles — takes any time between one and a half and eight days. When we make the journey and find ourselves grounded every few hours, tied up at night, lined up by strong ropes at critical points, and occasionally speeding backward with the current, we understand the margin allowed.

The boilers of river boats have to be very strong to stand the

75

pressure needed to fight against the swift current upward, while the descent is much more perilous because of the danger of losing control of the vessel and having it tossed helplessly about in the narrow, rocky canyons, or striking a snag and going to pieces.*

...One vessel took eight days in reaching Glenora, where she arrived with a thoroughly frightened lot of passengers who had, at various times, leaped into the water, jumped to the nearest rocks, sat with life-preservers fastened waiting for the boat to go to pieces, and spent dreadful hours when the boiler — an old one — panting under the undue pressure of steam, threatened an

Members of the Yukon Field Force on board the *Stikine Chief*.

---

* A fate which would certainly have befallen Fenton's boat, had it really found itself "occasionally speeding backward with the current", as she claimed in the previous paragraph.

explosion.

As we creep along— at a rate from six miles an hour to no miles plus a pride that we have not retrograded — we see Klondikers with their tow lines and crude, newly-built boats, wading up the shallow, rushing water, two men lining, two men rowing, or struggling over rocky banks with many a stumble, with hands and faces briar-torn, with clothing soaked and in tatters. One such party we passed — three men with a seventeen-foot boat in which a horse was standing, his four feet planted out firmly. He never moved; had he done so in this sweeping, rock-walled canyon through which we were passing, the entire party would have been drowned. It is nothing unusual for such a party to reach Glenora with one or more men missing on the way.

In winter it is worse, for a strong local wind, blowing fifty miles an hour sweeps down the river, making it a terrible, if not an impossible, thing for men or dogs to make headway up the ice against it. Men who heard of that fabled 'waggon road' over the Teslin trail started up the river in February, a long-continued procession over the ice, and suffered things in cold, storm and hardship that make the heart ache to hear.

In view of all this, the emphatically expressed opinion of all Canadian travellers on this route is that the British Columbia Government have done the best possible thing in contracting for an early continuation of the proposed Teslin Lake Railway from Telegraph Creek down to Port Simpson. This will bring the Yukon district within the safest, speediest and least expensive connection with the outside world. The Stikine River route to the goldfields is only a makeshift, and its time of service should be brief. There are too many difficulties on this river at all seasons of the year. The passage through alien territory and the manipulation of customs at Wrangel are something to wonder at, if they were not so utterly corrupt and outrageous. Then the river itself, by reason of its tremendous current, affords slow, expensive and dangerous navigation, while the constantly shifting sandbars prevent any definite channel route being marked.

...Fifty miles above the river mouth is the Grand Glacier, a vast arrested river of ice. It is about two miles in width and stretches down between sombre mountains some 3,500 feet high, widening at the mouth into a horseshoe sea, some ten miles in curve, of massive, dusty ice blocks. Our boat creeps around the bank of it — a terrible bank of crushed stone that has been forced down in this awful avalanche of centuries ago, and now fringes the great ice field. We look up the gleaming pathway, on and on to where it touches the horizon line fifty miles away. Nothing intervenes between the giant, jagged bed of blue ice and the bluer sky; only the dark wooded mountains on either side stand in sentinel relief. "The strength of the hills" is an awful and pitiless strength in the light of this resistless, crushing thing. On the opposite side of the river, not an eighth of a mile away, amid the soft greenery of cottonwood and fir, as if in very mockery of the icy avalanche, sprouts the hot steam of a boiling spring.

Faith Fenton writes a despatch for the *Globe*, protected from mosquitos by a headnet

Such grandeurs of nature are all around and above us, but at their feet lie gentler and more human things. The river shores are thickly wooded all the way with well-grown cottonwood and fir trees, and every few miles up the banks we pass settlements of campers. The first such settlement, some forty miles up, is a newly established customs post. It is on the boundary line and marks our entrance into Canadian territory again. There are trim shacks, still piney and white in their freshness, and some half-dozen tents. Two or three red-jacketed fellows wearing sombreros come down to the bank to greet their comrades-in-arms; they are members of the Mounted Police force who are temporarily in charge. Behind them are grouped some 25 campers, miners and woodmen, waiting a chance to get up the river. The little spot of human living is trim and neat, a most refreshing contrast to the shack town we left at the river mouth. Camp after camp we pass, some proclaiming by fresh-cut cordwood pile that they belong to woodmen who are cutting supplies for river steamers, others by their outfit telling that they are miners stopped by the break-up of the river ice and waiting the chance of a passing boat to go forward. There are men in canoes pulling hard up against the stream, and there are men lining up along the bank, dragging their heavily laden boats along just out of the current swirl. Last October there was never a sign of human life all the Stikine length, but now there are belated campers everywhere, with their faces all turned upstream and Klondike-ward.

Our force required three river boats but only two were obtainable, and as the Colonel did not deem it advisable to keep his men at Wrangel one hour longer than was necessary, the *Stikine Chief* and *Strathcona* divided our party between them, leaving the horses and remaining supplies, under Major Gardiner, to follow us as soon as possible, and our days of slow ascent up this most uncertain river passed pleasantly enough.

Each day of the four had its scenic beauties and incidents — the passing of the Grand Glacier, the high, granite-walled Little Canyon, so-called,* which we tumbled out on deck to view at 3 o'clock in the morning, while our teeth chattered until the Major ordered hot coffee; the various adventures of tie-ups, line-ups and groundings; the lost dog on the sandbar, the bear hunt that drew even the Colonel himself from his grave studies of the

---

* The Grand Canyon of the Stikine, quite impassable to boats of any kind, begins immediately above Telegraph Creek.

Teslin trail maps to climb the rocky heights and take a shot at the two bears who stalked, like slow-moving spots of black, high above us; the clean leap overboard of Private Steer to grasp the *Strathcona*'s boat that had loosed her moorings and was drifting rapidly down in the swift current, and the Colonel's "Good lad! good lad!" and the clappings that greeted the Winnipeg boy as he came to the surface and held on till he found bottom.

The Yukon Field Force, on the march

At night our soldier boys made the solitary places of our tie-ups mellow with guitar, mandolin, cornet, bugle and jolly choruses, until the fourth evening at sunset found us at rest before a village of tents and shacks, and the cheer that went up from those six hundred men in vari-fashioned attire was not for the red jackets but for the mail bags carried ashore— the first mail of the season.... . We had reached Glenora.

Glenora, June 10. ...When, on June 7th, orders reached the big Mackenzie-Mann outfit to permanently suspend operations to build a [rail] roadbed through to Teslin Lake, Glenora was stunned. The little village of tents paused in bewilderment, like a child that has received an undeserved blow, endeavouring to understand the situation.... Standing in knots upon the wharf and upon the bit of dusty white road beside the river, the miners —and there is hardly anyone else in Glenora — talked over the situation and decided to call an indignation meeting.... .

When the hour arrived there were nearly 2,000 men assembled.... . The tall forms of two or three members of the Mounted Police, conspicuous even among these men by their height as much as by scarlet jacket and sombrero, stood distinct among the throng, while here and there a woman listened from some outside vantage point. In the immediate background was the little village of tents, many having block lettered signs - "A Nugget Hotel", "Kamloops Restaurant", "Pack Train Office", "Laundry Done Here" (The fact that the said laundry is done at the rate of $3 per dozen does not appear).

...The outcome of the meeting was the unanimous passing of a resolution to be forwarded to the Provincial Government, and a copy to the Federal Government, which the *Globe* has doubtless already published: —

"Whereas the construction of the waggon road recently commenced from Glenora to Teslin Lake having been suddenly abandoned, we the citizens and free miners located at Glenora and Telegraph Creek, here in public meeting assembled this 7th day of June, 1898, declare extreme dissatisfaction with the action of the Government of the Dominion of Canada in advertising to Europe and elsewhere and advocating the Stikine route as the best road to the Yukon goldfields, with the promise of the completion of a waggon road from Glenora to Teslin Lake in the spring of the present year; and whereas no pack trail is adequate for the transportation of goods ready waiting at Glenora and Telegraph Creek, we pray, for the credit of British Columbia and the good of the Canadian route, that your Government will take immediate action for the completion of the before-named waggon road; and whereas there are some two of three thousand miners stranded at Glenora and Telegraph Creek, unable to proceed or return, we would respectfully urge upon your Government the desirability and necessity of instructing your representative here [James Parker, Government

Gold Commissioner] to at once employ these men at reasonable wages on the work of completing the waggon road to Teslin Lake."*

A number of the miners are selling their outfits and returning home. Others, with scant supplies and scanter bedding strapped upon their backs, are starting their weary way over the 150 mile-trail; but the larger portion are still waiting at Glenora... .

The little tent village by the Stikine is forlorn today. A wholesome, clean, healthy little village — so splendidly sane besides Wrangel-lying white upon the bank and bathed in the hot summer sun; for tents of discouraged miners are striking here and there, leaving ugly gaps in the long, curving, dusty roadway, while above it the plateau that for two weeks was gay with red coasts and bugle calls is left to solitude. They were good friends, the citizens, miners and soldiers, for those brief camping days. As the redcoats stepped gaily out in their daily routine march, with their packs upon their backs, their cry to the onlooking miners was, "Come right along, boys," and the answer never failed, "We'll be right after you."

But the last detachment of the Yukon Field Force had gone to follow the advance parties, which are already 15, 30, and 50 miles on the trail.

---

* This eminently sensible (and economical) suggestion was not acted upon.

EDWARD LESTER'S DIARY
"DAMN THE GOLDFIELDS ALTOGETHER"

Monday July 11th

Struck camp this morning at 7 a.m. in fine weather. We marched by sections, No. 4 Sect. leading, about 9 a.m. No. 3 followed about 9.30 & we (No. 2) started at 10.45, No. 1 bringing up the rear with Capt. Ogilvy & the Dr. We were, of course, in full marching order but were allowed to substitute the H[udson's] B[ay] 'tump-lines' for the 'Oliver' Equipment*, which most of us did. We marched at an easy pace to the five mile post, or Camp Wolseley, when we halted for lunch.

From here for the rest of the day's march it was a steady tramp up hill for eleven miles. The waggon road finished soon after passing Camp Wolseley & after that there is only a narrow trail, the ascent to the summit being made by a winding path cut in the face of the mountain in many places only a couple of feet wide. The sun was blazing hot but there was plenty of good water so we did not suffer much with thirst. Mr. Leduc was with our section & he did not overdo us as he gave us a short halt every hour.

We reached the summit about 4 o'clock & camped for the night on the bank of a little brook which winds its way towards a shallow lake about 200 yards off. As we were packed fifteen in a tent, Jack & I slept in the open air under a tarpaulin rolled in our blankets passed the night very snugly.

Tuesday July 12th

Reveille sounded at 5 a.m. & by 7.30 we were once more on

---

*Oliver equipment was a complicated leather harness of straps and buckles which supported the soldier's haversack, water bottle and side arms. There was no provision for a back pack. The British had tried Oliver equipment and rejected it in 1879-81, finding that the straps stretched in wet weather. Evans reported the equipment satisfactory, except that there were "too many straps which are easily lost" and the glass water bottles were too easily broken. Evans to Chief Staff Officer, Ottawa, 23 November 1899, in PAC, RG 9, II, B 1, Vol. 312. It was an experimental issue with the YFF in 1898 and Evans' comments may have contributed to its acceptance by the Canadian Militia, which retained it until 1914.

the move in the same order as before. The trail, which was only wide enough for us to march in single file, was all down hill till we reached the small Tahltan River which we did about 1 p.m. Here we halted for a short time & Mr. Leduc photographed a group of us resting near the log bridge which spans the river.

On leaving the Little Tahltan we had a steep summit to mount which took us some 30 to 40 minutes to climb, after which our way lay through a gloomy spruce forest with a dark looking lake on the left. After traversing this for some three or four miles, during which part of the march we suffered from the mosquitoes very much & also from shortness of water, we descended to the valley of the Tahltan & arrived at the camp about 2 p.m.

Wednesday July 13th

Orderly man. We had a rest today, having only a short fatigue in the morning. The river here swarms with salmon & trout & all hands are busy fishing. Fish is on the menu at every meal. I tried my luck in the afternoon & captured a fine trout weighing about 4 lbs. I also hooked another about the same size but he broke away & I lost him. However the one I had furnished a good supper for Platt & I, so I was satisfied. We went out again in the evening but the fish were off the feed & as the mosquitoes were decidedly on we did not try for long. Some of the left half-coy. managed to gaff a fine salmon about 30 lb weight.

Thursday July 14th

Sergts. Mess fatigue. Fine morning. Drill order at 10 a.m. but did not drill. Lecture by Colour-Sgt. Davies re discipline, etc. Occupied rest of morning carpeting floor of tent with pine tops. No. 2 Coy. not in yet.

Our camp is very pleasantly situated on the banks of the Tahltan river, which is a swiftly running mountain stream of pure sweet water at present abounding in salmon & trout, the latter running very large, sometimes as high as four pounds. There is plenty of wood & water handy, & in fact we are very comfortable but for the mosquitoes who are an awful pest &

torment the life out of us; they will bite through anything, even through our serge trousers.* The whole of No. 3 Company is at present in camp here, & also a part of No.1 together with two of the nurses, Miss Faith Fenton, Dr. Foster, Capts. Ogilvy & Bennett, & Lt. Leduc. We are expecting No. 2 with the Major & Capt. Thacker but they have not yet put in an appearance. I went out this morning to try & get a couple of trout for breakfast but the mosquitoes were so thick that I was glad to beat a retreat. I have been reading the *Tragedy of the Korosco* by Conan Doyle & am now reading the *Scallywag* by Grant Allen. Wet evening.

Friday July 15th

Working guard. Raining all night. Could not go fishing myself so lent Spence rod & line. He was absent about an hour & returned with two fine trout one weighing about 3 1/2 lbs & one about a pound less. In the evening he brought in another three pounder, so supper & breakfast are safe. At 8 p.m. No. 2 Coy. marched into camp. The rain had cleared off but it still looks threatening. They have been three days on the march, having only marched as far as Camp Wolseley the first day.

Saturday July 16th

Mounted guard at 9 a.m. with Spence & Betts, Corp. Coupe in charge. No. 2 Coy. brought in the mail & I received a letter from my mother enclosing, much to my astonishment, one from Ethel Jarrey. She begs me to write to her. This on first thoughts I decided not to do, at all events directly, but on second thoughts I don't see why I should not do so for I do not think for a moment she would let out my whereabouts to M. if I asked her not to; & even if she did let it out, what harm could it do me out in this country?** Yes! I think I shall write, her letters will be some-

---

* "In the morning a pack train went ahead with our baggage and Miss Payson and I started off on foot. The mosquitoes were so thick Sergeant Batemen's red coat was brown with them. We had to stuff the openings in our gautlets, with paper, and not stopping for lunch, hold a piece of food inside our veil and eat as we walked." — "Rachel Hanna's Diary", in *Bracebridge Herald-Gazette*, 11 April 1974.

** It seems likely that 'M' was Lester's estranged wife, and probably the reason for his emigration to Canada and enlistment under a false name.

thing else to look forward to at all events. She is at present in business with Bonthson & Co., 52 Glasshouse St., Regent St., & is 20 years old.

My mother tells me that Ada has presented Arthur with a son & heir. The event came off on the 7th June.

Some of the boys were out this afternoon fishing & returned with no less than 13 salmon, the smallest weighing at least 20 lb, the largest being 40 to 50 lbs or even more. These were all taken with the gaff inside of 3 or 4 hours. No. 2 Coy. marched for the next post this afternoon. The boys got 12 more salmon in the evening.

I have seen some 'Okeeless'* since I have been in this country but tonight they beat all I ever saw. It was absolutely impossible to rest a minute from 4 to 9 p.m. after which they let up somewhat. It started raining about 9 o'clock & continued all night.

Sunday July 17th

Dismounted guard at 9 a.m. and a more miserable guard I never wish to put in, what with the rain & the mosquitoes. The guard tent was flooded. I call it a tent by courtesy but it was only a canvas sheet thrown over a pole at each end. However, we kept up a warming fire in spite of the rain & as we had plenty of tea, boiled salmon & 'hardtack' we managed to make ourselves as comfortable as possible under the circumstances. It continued to rain heavily all day & there were no Church parades. Nearly all the tents in the lines were flooded excepting ours which has up to now kept perfectly dry.

Monday July 18th

Rained heavily all night & continued all day. No parades. Issued with oil-skin coats. Forty men to march out tomorrow. They will consist of the Right half of No. 3 Coy. the remainder to be made up of the remnants of Nos. 1 & 2 Coys. left in camp.

---

* Presumably an Indian word for mosquitoes.

Tuesday July 19th

As the rain still continued, the start was postponed till finer. It cleared up about 11 a.m. so we shifted the tents back & [illegible] everything. This evening we are all busy preparing for an early start tomorrow. A big pack train came in this afternoon with an escort of two men & a prisoner. They brought in some mail but there was none for me.

In a *Montreal Herald* of June 18th it stated that Pte. Thos. Robinson, RRCI, of St. Johns, Quebec, had been sent to a lunatic asylum, insane from the effects of too much cigarette smoking.

It still keeps fine & looking all right for tomorrow.

Wednesday July 20th

The morning dawned dull & cloudy & threatened rain which began to fall again about 8.30 a.m. We made a start about 11 o'clock in a pouring rain & a queer looking lot we must have looked, not much like the smart crowd that marched through Ottawa some two months ago. We were dressed in our yellow oilskin jackets & blue jean overalls, the whole surmounted by our helmets more or less the worse for wear.* The trail was now much more difficult & as we were escorting a train of pack mules our progress was necessarily very slow. The trail followed for some distance the course of the river, sometimes on the level & sometimes high above, along the face of rocky bluffs, through forests & over swamps, but everywhere there was mud, in many places half way up to our knees, & we were unable to do more than two or two & a half miles an hour.

We only marched about eight miles & then halted at a clearing in the forest for the night. We pitched our tents in a good spot but as there were only two for the whole crowd J.P. & I decided to sleep out, so we rigged a little shelter tent of two rubber sheets & with our blankets hope to sleep pretty comfortable, please God & the mosquitoes. We march early tomorrow & hope to make the Hudson Bay Post (20 miles). It has stopped raining & is now fair.

---

* In his popular history, *Klondike: The Life and Death of the Last Great Gold Rush*, (Toronto; 1958), Pierre Berton has the troops marching along in "scarlet jackets and white helmets — marching as best they could in close order ... trudging in step through the mud holes and over rocks and stumps."

A pack train making its way up the steep bank of the Stikine river, leaving Telegraph Creek

Thursday July 21st

We struck camp this morning at 9 o'clock & made a start at 9.15. We did about 18 or 19 miles, only halting once for about 15 minutes. The trail was if anything in a worse condition than yesterday & we had a lot of difficulties to overcome; consequently our progress was again very slow. About a mile from the start we came to a large lake, about three miles in length, after which the way lay along the margin of a chain of lakes, sometimes along the very margin & sometimes hundreds of feet up, now running through the depths of a forest, now through a gloomy gorge with beetling crags overhead, now crossing a mountain torrent, now winding over a shaking bog, over a corduroy road a slip from which meant a plunge to the knees in black peaty slime.

However the longest lane has a turning & the longest march an end, & at 4.30 the H.B. post hove in sight (45 miles from Telegraph) where No. 2 Coy. & some of No. 1 were encamped. The cooks of No. 2 Coy. had some hot tea with beef & biscuits ready for us & never did a meal taste better than that did to us who had nothing but a couple of biscuits & a slice of bully beef since our early breakfast. This evening I sent a letter to Ethel by some of the packers who were going back to Glenora. As our section tent is too crowded Platt, Lawsen, Thompson, McGowan, Lefebvre & myself were put into one of No. 1 Coy.'s tents. We are eleven in all, Gareau is in charge & Brunette, who used to be at St. Johns, is also in the tent.

Friday July 22nd

It rained all day but cleared up in the evening. This is the best piece of camping ground we have had yet, being good & dry, consisting of a flat of three or four acres entirely enclosed by mountain peaks, capped with perpetual snow & enveloped in clouds during the present damp weather. The river on the bank of which the camp is situated is a branch of the Sheslay. It is no more than a mountain torrent, hardly worthy of the name of a river, but nevertheless abounds in salmon & trout.

Our amusements in camp are rather limited being confined to tip-cat & quoits, with horseshoes. It is with the former highly intellectual game that I have been amusing myself this evening. There is a tobacco famine in camp, all the tobacco having all gone on with earlier parties, but Jack & I have enough to last us about a week with care.

The Officers here are Capt. Thacker, Capt. Bennett & Lt. Leduc. The Dr. also rode into camp today. The women have not come in yet which is a blessing, as in the other camp they were an infernal nuisance their tents being so close to ours that they could overhear all that went on, & they were continually making complaints, Tommy's language not being always of the choicest. If they were so very modest they should have had their tents pitched away from our lines, as they were at Telegraph where there was no trouble. I think Faith Fenton is at the bottom of it all.

Saturday July 23rd

Kit inspection for No. 3 Coy. at 2 p.m. Only No. 3 [Coy.] of course. Fine morning but rain in the afternoon. There's an Indian encampment near our lines but we cannot visit it as it has been put out of bounds. There is one old chap there who they claim to be over 100 years old. I have seen him & I believe it. I should say he was a thousand. He still speaks of white men as "King George's men". There is one young Indian who speaks some little English & comes up to the camp sometimes for a chat with the boys. He is quite a masher & wears a white collar & a tie.

It has rained more or less now since the 14th, mostly more. This must either be the rainy season or we have struck a 'wet belt'.* The tobacco famine is now a thing of the past, as a pack train came in today bringing in 8 cases & each man was served out with a plug. Occupied the evening playing tip-cat on scientific principles & after played a rubber of whist. Each tent was issued with a candle this evening as the days are beginning to draw in & it is pretty well dark by 'first post'. Soap is getting scarce & our last issue was one bar per tent.

Sunday July 24th

No service of any kind & we have been pretty much confined to our tents all day by the rain. We mount the usual quarter

---

* A letter from Sergeant Rhoades, RCD, (who was with Colonel Evans and the advance party) reported that "the soldiers found the road from Telegraph Creek to Teslin Lake rougher than could be imagined. They only covered eight miles a day for 30 days. During this period they had steady rain for a week." — *Winnipeg Daily Tribune*, 30 July 1898.

guard of three men but mount in fatigue dress.

The woods around swarm with squirrels but otherwise seem destitute of animal life. There is however a profusion of wild flowers which are much the same as those of the Stikine district. Amongst other I noticed the monkshood or aconite & another blue spike something like it, the name of which I just now forget but remember seeing it as a boy in the old garden at Rochester. There are also plenty of lupins & dog violets. We have gathered also plenty of wild gooseberries & red currants & I have heard of some black currants & raspberries being found.

The health of the troops is excellent & there have been only two cases of rheumatism, one of which was sent home from the Tahltan. There has been no sickness at all amongst the St. John's men.

Monday July 25th

No rain today. On fatigue getting wood for the cooks in the morning. Our section under Sgt. Lapierre is to march tomorrow with a pack train to establish a forwarding post three days march from here.

Tuesday July 26th

Struck our tent at 9 a.m. & marched out, ten men under Sgt. Lapierre at 9.40. Our party consists of Sgt. Lapierre, Arnott, Cox, Doré, Graham, Hayes, Lowe, Platt, Spence, Dumas & myself. We crossed the river soon after we left camp & immediately began the ascent of what is known as the Hudson Bay Summit. We climbed & climbed for three solid hours, not a gradual ascent but real hard collar work, all the time the pack train in front, ploughing through stiff mud over our ankles & stumbling over loose rocks till at last we reached the summit where we halted for a spell, but the air was too bitterly cold to stay long & we were glad to make a start again. After marching about a couple of miles we again halted & camped for the night. Although we were nearly five hours marching we have only made six miles, but are at an altitude of 3600 ft, the H.B. post being 1850 ft, so we have ascended about 1750 ft since we started.

Our campground is very bad, being in the middle of a short thick bush, near a pool of stagnant water which is the best we can get to drink & is full of wigglers & pollywogs. We have, however, cleared a space for the tent & spread pine tops on the floor. We have also built a huge camp fire, for which there is plenty of material handy & which serves the double purpose of keeping us warm & driving away the mosquitoes, & as we have plenty of tea, sugar, beef, & hard tack we are not altogether uncomfortable.

The Dr. & Major Young joined us on horseback soon after we halted & will remain with us till we reach our destination, which is called 'Cache Creek', & will then return to [the] H.B. post. Our course tomorrow will run due north & will be, I believe, pretty level, so I believe we are in for a long march. I was not very well during today's march, having a headache & a faint feeling, & I was afraid I was in for a touch of fever, but after a good can of tea & a snooze this afternoon I feel all right this evening.

Wednesday July 27th

Twenty good miles today, over a pretty level trail as trails go in this part of the world, & the trail in fairly good condition. The scenery was the prettiest we have yet passed through during our march. But we did not come across so many streams & suffered somewhat from thirst.

The place we are camped in is very swampy but we had to stop here as this is the farthest point to which the road makers have gone & we are camping near them. Right ahead is a boggy place which will have to be corduroyed before the mule train can cross. We have pitched our tent on a knoll of high ground & so are pretty dry. We have only four or five miles to do tomorrow.

Thursday July 28th

We had to wait whilst the corduroying mentioned above was finished so made a rather late start. The trail today lay through a low bush & dry swamp, very easy marching & down hill or level. We were joined by three pack trains all bound for Cache Creek. One of them was in charge of a man who we found out was half-brother to McGowan.

We arrived at our destination after about two hours marching & found an ideal camping ground on a grassy hillside with good water within easy reach. After unloading & getting dinner we had an afternoon's work making a Q.M. store out of the bags & boxes. We then constructed a marquee for ourselves, giving our tent to the Dr. who is not going back with the Major. The latter returns tomorrow.

Spence was unanimously elected cook.

Friday July 29th

The Major returned today, so the Dr. is the only officer with us & he don't count. Consequently we are having a regular picnic. We did a little work this morning building an Officer's latrine & we are going to build one for ourselves tonight. We do not expect any more troops in till Tuesday. It is a glorious day & very hot. We got some mail on one of the [pack] trains & I got two lots of Manchester papers & *Tid Bits*, * also 4 numbers of *Short Stories*. We can get all we want to eat & plenty of reading matter so we are OK. After supper which consisted of tea, without milk of course, but with plenty of sugar, fried 'bully beef', stewed apricots, & damper, or bannocks, we went to work again building another latrine & setting up one of the portable stoves for the cook.

Saturday July 30th

We have named this place Fort Douglass [sic] in honour of Maj. Young & have put a sign up to that effect. The following is the menu for the day

Breakfast
Fried Bully Beef
Stewed Apricots
Buns
Tea
Dinner

---

* A British weekly journal of the time.

Bully Beef
Fried Onions
Apricot Pie
Buns

<u>Supper</u>
Pork & Beans
Apricots
Buns
Tea

How's that for a bush bill of fare. Dumas is cook, *vice* Spence, resigned. Today we secured 15 lb of fresh beef from the road makers who are camped about a mile behind us. Steak & onions for breakfast tomorrow.

A campground on the Teslin trail

Sunday July 31st

Today has been a day of rest, in deed as well as in name; we have done absolutely nothing but eat, drink, smoke & read all day long. We had beef steaks for breakfast & dinner, & pancakes for supper. I was on guard last night with Hayes. Guard simply consists of taking your blankets & sleeping in the Stores. There was a pack train in today which left the post on Friday. All hands had a bath in the stream or creek this afternoon; the water was icy cold & we were not long in getting out again.

We have had no rain since reaching here & the days are fine & warm but it is very cold at night.

Monday August 1st

Today passed uneventfully except for a revolt of the cooks. Consequently each one had to cook his own dinner & truly variety was the order of this day. The difficulty was however adjusted & things are running smoothly again.

We hear that the remainder of No. 3 Coy. are on the trail & will probably be in tomorrow.

Tuesday August 2nd

The balance of No. 3 Coy. marched in this morning before we had got breakfast. They brought in some mail with them. I got three lots of *Manchester W[eekly] T[imes]* & *Tid Bits*, also a *Regiment* of June 2nd, but no letters. They certainly don't over exert themselves at home in the way of correspondence & as for Cotton! Well, he's past praying for.

There is a rare fuss being made in the various Canadian papers about the so-called 'mutiny' at Glenora & there has, in every case, been gross exaggeration of the one or two cases of insubordination on the part of two or three men, but these reports are doing a great deal of mischief & are calculated to bring a great deal of discredit on the Permanent Force.* These false reports should certainly be contradicted, if not through the press, at all events by individuals in their private letters.

Wednesday August 3rd

Maj. Young came in yesterday, & Wesley, who slept in our

---

* Evans had a poor opinion of the Interior Department men. They were "a distinct drawback to the Force and subversive to discipline. The majority of this party appeared to consider it the duty of the soldiers to wait upon them, and of the Government to feed them better than it did the Officers, N.C. Officers and Men of the Force, and when this was not done their discontent took the form of writing lying letters to Newspapers and Others." — Evans to Adjutant-General, 1 November 1898, in D Hist 73/78.

tent. We had a short fatigue this morning, our section being detailed to get wood for the cooks; as they had plenty we retired gracefully to our canvas mansion. The weather still continues fine but, alas, our picnic is over & we are once more on 'bully beef & hard tack'.

I hear that a party is to march out tomorrow.

Thursday August 4th

Pack train in today which goes on tomorrow accompanied by four men & Corp. Hansen. Fatigue this morning, making a latrine for the nurses who, however, have not yet arrived.

The lead packer of the newly arrived train & Capt. Ogilvy got to loggerheads about something or other & the packers were all bundled out of our lines. Capt. Ogilvy altered the name of the post to 'Fort Evans'.

Friday August 5th

Corp. Hansen with Rogers, Tansley, Langille & Bell left with a pack train this morning. Three trains came in today with a detachment of the Artillery, who are camped three or four hundred yards from us down the trail. No. 2 Coy. expected this evening. Drs. Inspection at 2 p.m.

This afternoon we were all in the tent, some playing cards, some reading & others, amongst these myself, asleep, when suddenly a whirlwind swept the canvas of the tent completely away from the framework. Well, you ought to have seen the stampede, for we thought the heavy poles would be about our ears. Papers, cards, etc., were all scattered & whisked up into the air, one newspaper being carried up two or three hundred feet. However, there was no damage done & we soon righted matters.

Twelve men picked from No. 3 Coy. are to start tomorrow under Capt. Ogilvy to march right through to Teslin lake. Platt, Lowe & myself are the only ones from the left half who have been picked. No. 2 Coy. came in this evening & brought some mail. I got some papers, in one parcel of which were enclosed six lead pencils. They had been discovered at Glenora & the Postmaster sent word by Cockburn not to let it occur again.*

Saturday August 6th

When we rose this morning we found there had been a sharp frost during the night & several articles which had been put out to dry were frozen stiff. We did not make a start till 3 p.m. on account of the pack train [not] being ready. We marched easily & made seven or eight miles, camping for the night in a small gully near a stream. The night was very cold & there was a sharp frost again.

Sunday August 7th

We made an early start ahead of the pack train. We marched for two & a half hours, making about ten miles here. We rested during the heat of the day, getting lunch & waiting for the train to overtake us, which it did about an hour, then made another start & after marching another three hours halted about a mile beyond Mackenzie & Mann's camp where we obtained some fresh beef. Just after passing the above, and about half a mile before reaching our own campground, I had a slight attack of vertigo from the sun. We camped amongst the trees & after a good hot cup of tea & some beef soup I soon felt all right again.

We expect to reach the Nahlin River tomorrow.

Monday August 8th

We were unable to make a start this morning on account of losing three of our mules. We got off, however, at last, marching as usual ahead of the train and letting a couple of men stay behind to help the packers. We marched about five miles & then halted for the train to overtake us. They failed, however, to put in an appearance till after 2 p.m. We let them pass, sending the

* The postmaster was probably not well disposed towards the Force and happy to enforce the letter of the law. Colonel Evans and he had clashed in June when: "Shortly after the arrival of the Pack Train with the mail, I proceeded to town [Telegraph Creek] and found a large crowd of men gathered in and about a small tent known as a hotel, where letters were being sorted and delivered by one J. McKay at the rate of $0.25 per letter. He informed me that he had arranged with the Postmaster at Glenora, his partner in business, to carry the mail to Teslin, charge $0.25 per letter, and divide the proceeds. Knowing this act to be unjust and illegal, I took possession of the mail and compelled him to refund to the public the amounts already collected." A party of NCO's and men then sorted and delivered the mail. — Evans to Adjutant-General, 14 July 1898, in PAC, RG 9, A1, Vol. 417, ff 17040.

two cooks ahead with them. An hour after we made a start, but had not marched more than half a mile when we met the two cooks returning, who informed us that the train was coming back to camp in the place we had just left on account of some of the mules showing signs of distress; so back we had to go & here we were only five miles further than we were last night.

This is more annoying as we know that Capt. Thacker & No. 2 Coy. is not far behind, i.e. at our last night's camping place. We are determined, however, to make an early start tomorrow & six of us have volunteered to get up & hunt the mules up, & also help drive the train along so we can hustle the mules & get over more ground. Then instead of camping at the Nahlin we can get some seven or eight miles beyond. By that means we hope to still keep our lead of No. 2 Company.

The weather is much warmer & there has been a blazing sun all day.

Tuesday August 9th

Man proposes etc., and "The best laid scheme of mice & men oft gang agley." Today has been one of many disappointments. We were up bright & early & were out hunting up the mules before 3 a.m. but, alas, we did not find them all. At 6 o'clock we had them all but three, but search as we might at 1.30 p.m. we had only two more, the other we lost entirely. Then our chief packer was taken sick & with one thing & another we had to make up our minds for another night here. To fill up our cup of bitterness No. 2 Coy. pass through about 11 o'clock & jeer to their hearts content. Cap. Ogilvy swears we will yet beat them into Teslin & we intend to back him up if it kills us.

Wednesday August 10th

We got the mules together earlier this morning & made a start about 10 a.m. Six of us acted as mule leaders but in spite of this we were only able to make the Nahlin River, on account of the horrible state of the trail which was rough & boggy. For miles we journeyed through what we called the white forest. This white forest was once black as any of the fire-swept woods, but time & winter snows have cleansed every trunk to a peculiar whiteness & there they stand, a forest of tall white ghosts with green underbush about their feet.

The mule I was leading was a perfect devil. If we stopped a moment he'd lie down &, when moving, he used to try & walk up my back & several time trod on my heels, & a mule treading on your heels, I tell you, is no joke.

The Nahlin is a swift mountain stream very much like the Tahltan &, like it, is crossed by a log bridge. Where we are camped it runs between high bluffs but between them & the river is a level stretch of green sward & on this our tents are pitched. We all had a bathe in the cold mountain water & felt much refreshed.

During the night we heard a familiar voice sing out in stentorian tones. It was Dumas going through, acting as packer to one of Durrant's trains.

Thursday August 11th

The train made an early start this morning & we set off about half an hour after. We first had to climb the steep bluff overlooking the river which gave us three quarters of an hour's steady climb. Here we rested a few minutes & then set off at a rattling pace over a fair trail passing the train with which Dumas was not yet [illegible] up. We overtook the train after doing about 2 1/2 miles. Here we rested to let the train get on again & then made a fresh start. The trail now began to get very rough & uneven with large tracts of spongy bog every now & again, & mostly up hill. After a few miles of this we halted for lunch. After this the trail got worse & worse, though some of the soft parts were corduroyed for a quarter of a mile or more at a stretch.

Bye & bye we sighted a large lake, Lake Victoria, or Little Fish Lake in the Indian language, along the low hills fringing the margin of which the trail ran. The lake is some six miles long & a mile broad, & half way along its shore we halted for the night having made ten miles or so. There are plenty of wild fowl on the lake but though we could easily shoot them we could not get them without a boat. As soon as we got the camp fixed all hands plunged into the lake & enjoyed a good swim which refreshed us all very much. Have seen or heard nothing of No. 2 Coy.

Friday August 12th

We had the hardest march of the whole trip today. The sun has been scorching hot & the trail almost all up hill. We crossed one mountain (Rainy Mount), the summit of which took us an hour's hard climbing to reach, & to make matters worse it was literally a mountain of bog. The trail was something horrible, swamp, swamp, swamp, all the way along & very little corduroy after the first few miles. We passed Corp. Hansen & party soon after the start & for nearly the whole of the rest of the distance we were floundering through bog, scrambling over tree roots & fallen logs, here & there coming across a mud hole in which the mules sank to their girths & from which they had to be hauled by main strength.

For a couple of miles or more we passed through the smouldering ashes of what must have been a terrible forest fire only a few hours before, as it was still burning in many places as we passed, & the hot ashes scorched our feet & made the heat something terrific. We halted at mid-day to allow the heat of the day to pass. We stayed for about four hours on the edge of a small lake about a mile in length, the margin of which was so swampy that we could not reach it & the only water we could get was from under the roots of a tree & this smelt & tasted strongly of sulphur. Meanwhile the fire had broken out again behind us & dense clouds of smoke covered the sky behind & to our right. The wind luckily was in the opposite direction but for a time we had great fears for the train which, however, arrived safely & we made another start, this time following the mules, as we were uncertain where the packers intended to camp.

With all our difficulties, however, we have managed to make thirteen or fourteen miles & are camped in a good place somewhere off the trail. It is grassy but there is too much bush about to pitch more than one tent so we are sleeping "Under the canopy of heaven". I don't think No. 2 Company are far ahead although reports along the trail are very conflicting. We are constantly meeting & overtaking parties who are packing their stuff by relays & there must be hundreds of tons on the trail.

Saturday August 13th

Whilst we were preparing for a start this morning we heard the bugle of No. 2 Coy. sounding Reveille, so we knew our rivals were not far ahead, though how far it was hard to tell as the air was very still. We had a rattling good march over a fairly good trail & not much hill climbing. After marching about three miles we sighted a fine sheet of water called Moose Lake, about eight miles long by one broad, along the shore of which we marched. About three miles from the end we came upon No. 2 Coy. camped for the night. We passed right through their camp to our huge delight & camped about a mile and a half beyond them. We have now got the lead once more & intend to try & keep it into Teslin, which we hope to reach on Monday night or Tuesday morning. We are right out of tobacco & some of the boys are smoking scraped willow bark.

There is a split in the trail for tomorrow, a new trail is being made which will cut off a considerable number of miles, but we intend to take the old trail as we are not certain that the new one is yet completed & we do not wish to have to break a new trail for ourselves.

Sunday August 14th

We had another good march today over an easy trail. The advanced party of No. 2 Coy, composed of Artillery under Capt. Bennett, passed through our camp before we started but we soon overtook them resting. As determined yesterday we took the old trail & camped for the night in a very swampy place on the edge of a shallow stream which the advance party have named Shallow Creek. The stream runs out of a lake which is quite near & has a good sandy bottom; in this we enjoyed a good swim. We cannot tell whether or not we are ahead of No. 2 as the other trail joins this some six miles on ahead.

Monday August 15th

Today has been a great day & a record march. We made a start good & early, & soon ascertained that we were still ahead of No. 2. We marched rapidly but the trail was simply awful with swamps & bush fires; we had to pass through one part with the trees burning on either side & the heat was terrific. About noon we halted near a creek with a very bad crossing. After a time we sighted No. 2 in the distance & Cap. Ogilvy determined on a piece of strategy which was apparently rewarded with complete success. We unpacked the mules & made all preparations as if camping for the night & quietly waited till No. 2 came past, looking as crestfallen as possible. They sucked it in beautifully & marched past us, a self-satisfied grin upon most countenances. We felt certain that they fully believed we should not move again that day.

About 2 o'clock we saddled up again & off we went. We marched 22 miles on end making 28 miles in all. About 6 o'clock we marched through No. 2 camp to their unbounded amazement. We put on a swinging pace, although to tell the truth we were all thoroughly done in. However, we marched or rather crawled another five miles, making, as said above, 28 miles in all, & that over as bad a bit of trail as it has yet been my luck to see. We are 4 1/2 miles from Teslin Lake, camped in the forest near a portage of the Teslin river.

Tuesday August 16th

We were up before dawn this morning & started off at daybreak for we were afraid the other Company would try & steal a march on us in the small hours of the morning. This, as a matter of fact, they did, but we had the start of them & marched triumphantly into camp at 7 a.m. No. 2 arrived about 2 p.m. or seven hours behind us. The following verse was written on a "blazed" tree by the side of the trail.

Damn the journey, Damn the track,
Damn the distance there & back,
Damn the sunshine, Damn the weather,
Damn the Goldfields altogether.

Now that we are at last safely at the end of our long & difficult march it might be as well to give a brief resume of the journey & some of my impressions, by the way, of the Teslin trail on the whole.

The fairly good, & in some places excellent, condition of the first hundred miles of the trail, affords a great contrast to that of the remaining distance. I may here state by the way that all travellers over the trail & also the packers assert that it exceeds the 130 miles usually stated in the so-called guide books. Probably from 175 to 180 miles is a fair average. But whether this last portion of the trail be 50 or 75 miles all agree that it has not one redeeming feature.

To anyone who has lived his or her life in the eastern part of Canada, the country traversed by this part of the trail is unique. The word "bog" usually conveys to the average mind the idea of a low-lying marshy level. Here it means hill-land, not merely covered with moss but absolutely composed of it. Not, however, the soft velvety article the word usually indicates, but a spongy, yielding stuff, a fibrous conglomeration of roots, dead grass & decaying wood, topped by a thick, yellowish-green moss, very coarse & harsh to the touch. There is little or no soil properly speaking, but this substance extends down from one to three feet & below this, summer & winter, solid ice.

We came across this state of things immediately after crossing the Nahlin River. The river is the largest on the trail & may be said to form the chief divisional point of the whole march. As it cannot be forded it is spanned, like the Tahltan, by a really excellent log bridge.

If the Nahlin were a mountain range it could hardly be a more complete dividing line. The entire aspect of the country changes after crossing it. To the south the trail passes through a mountainous region intersected every few miles with shallow, brawling streams of clear, ice-cold water. The tablelands resemble bits of wild park with beautiful blue mountain lakes. We catch glimpses of loftier mountain heights & we look down into wooded ravines & glades. It is high & dry, hot days & cold nights, up & down, ascent & descent, a mountain trail with mountain scenery.

Beyond the river, what a contrast! The trail traverses an undiscovered country, so to speak: a hill bog-land & a hill log-land alternately. It is either bog or log all the way. To explain, we are either tramping through the bog moss, beaten by the feet of many pack mules into black unfathomable depths, or with equal difficulty scrambling, crawling, making our way over miles upon miles of ground blackened by prostrate logs. We are passing through a country of skeleton trees. To the south of the Nahlin we see the trees beautiful in their natural verdure, but all the rest of the way lies through forests of half-dead, half-hearted trees or trunks, stripped & blackened by prostrate logs. Sometimes our way lay for miles & miles through blackened, smoking trees & over bogs yet licked by tongues of flame, tracing the trail as best we could over the hot, smoking ashes, whilst the crash of falling trees added to the intensity of the situation. Only those who have undergone the experience can realize the depressing effect of the journey over a burnt-out track of ashes, blackness, & desolation.

Alternating with all this came spells of bog travelling which is a more serious matter, at all events from a packer's point of view. This 'soft land' begins in real earnest about 40 to 50 miles south of Teslin, intersected here & there by ridges of solid ground. Gazing round from a vantage point on one of these ridges, we see on either side of us, as far as the eye can reach, nothing but low-lying bog. For miles around us on either side there is only bog of various degrees of stability, here & there dry & crisp, but more often wet & spongy. This view is bounded far on the left by high mountains, & away on the other hand by a stagnant, swampy lake, unapproachable for [because of?] bog. The wet, swampy moss almost invariably centres to a perfect slough of despond in which our unfortunate pack mules sink to the girths. Once more I cannot help again referring to the very curious feature of this country, that this bog is not necessarily confined to low-lying land but rather it belongs to the hills.

A great deal of corduroying has been done, & stretches of over a quarter of a mile bridge many of the soft spots, but this corduroy is not lasting. We experienced many instances of this in corduroy laid early in the season, perhaps by inexperienced hands. The bog had worked into deep holes at either end, the logs had shifted & huge gaps formed in the surface, this, with the loose shifting logs, rendering the whole thing highly danger-ous both to man & beast; & in many places it had been flung aside by the desperate packers who preferred braving the dangers of the boggy spot to risking their animals' legs on the obnoxious corduroy.

The important query is, can this trail be made enduring? To my mind, lacking of course, technical knowledge, it can not; there appears to be no solid basis on which to rest any surface work. This spongy substance has no staying power & is subject to the action of the ice beneath, & unless the corduroy be built on stilts or hills it appears to me that the frost & ice of one winter would tear it all apart. However, by my opinion worth what it may, it is certain that nothing but costly & arduous work can ever place the last fifty miles of the Teslin trail in anything like a permanently good condition.

FAITH FENTON'S & GEORGIA POWELL'S DESPATCHES

"FROM MOUNTAIN TO SWAMP AND BOG"

Telegraph Creek, June 28 - When a brigade is covering new ground in a series of detachments, as in the instance of the Yukon force, there are only two positions for a correspondent: either with the advance column or at the base. Each guard has its advantages. The former undergoes those first ventures and experiences so dear to every journalistic heart, while the latter enjoys a more comprehensive, if not a fuller, knowledge. The base holds the key that taps information all long the line. It is the point of communication with the outside world. To it is entrusted the responsible work of forwarding the needful food and medical supplies, as well as all mail and special communications. And it is upon the watchful care of the base that the various advance detachments are relying as they travel forward day by day further from the resources of civilisation.

Thus, we who are stationed for a time at the trail entrance have continually before us a vision of the detachments marching ahead: the resolute Colonel and his [advance] guard to the forefront; the plucky little feminine triad [Nurses Powell and Scott and Mrs. Starnes] but a day or two's journey in their rear; the stout Major [Bliss or Talbot?] hastening solitary from base to join the advance; the Captains with their encampments between; the nurses keeping watch over the waylaid sick man, and the long continuous line of pack trains moving slowly on.

All these are ours. Company after company, in stout marching gear have left us to face the long tramp over the narrow way. Passing trail travellers bring us news of their faring: messengers come back at intervals with orders or requirements from the far advance, but concerning the details of the journey we shall know nothing until we assemble once more a complete force, at Fort Selkirk.

We who are at the base will move slowly, for not a pound of supplies must be left behind, and packing is but slow transportation. Only when the last load is lifted and carried, swinging, up the trail behind the tinkling mule leader will the rear column strike its tents and move up the narrow way.

For there is no royal road to Teslin Lake — not as yet. Transportation companies may advertise beautiful things, and pack-train owners talk glibly, but there is no escape from the trail for either millionaire or tramp miner. The former may ride his horse; the latter shoulder his pack and foot the weary way. Yet over many of the miles walking is preferable to riding and the hum of the mosquito is over it all. They are endurable here — at the trail entrance — these vampires among insects. With protecting mosquito veil and gloves worn through morning and evening hours we live in modest comfort, for the hills are not their chosen places. But ominous reports come back to us from the low and swampy place of the trail— reports which we are in no haste to verify by personal experience.

It is one of the many entertaining things as we wait here and a source of never-failing amusement, to watch the operation of loading a 'green' mule pack. Mules are used in preference to horses, being surer footed, steadier and stronger on the trail. A mule's strength seems to lie in his back and legs, since he has little drawing power.

The alert, saucy, slender young animals are in the corral — a roughly-fenced enclosure belonging to some one of the several packers over the trail. Leaning indolently on the fence are various easily-attired men, perhaps the owners of the load lying in piled heaps near at hand; perhaps some old adepts in packing in search of a new 'wrinkle' for packing for the trail is an art, and the best packer in the district is not only a man of fame, but a millionaire to boot.

The load has already been weighed and sorted , so many pounds for each animal. It consists of boxes, bags, rolls and anomalous articles of all sorts that go to make up a miner's outfit. Whether an animal can carry 200, 300, or even 400 pounds depends largely on the shape of the load. A packer abhors boxes and cumbrous articles; he would have everything in bags, since they adjust more easily to the animal's back. A mule bearing 150 pounds in boxes and light but cumbrous articles may be fully loaded, while another can carry twice as

Packers lash a load on a patient mule, somewhere along the trail

much in bags. With packing rates at forty cents per pound, the reason for the preference is clear.

A young mule is brought up near the load, led by halter and blinded [blindfolded]. His ears are alert, his nostrils slightly distended. He is patted and soothed, but careens suspiciously away. A folded blanket is placed cushion-wise on his back, fastened with a surcingle, and over this the *aprarjos* (pronounced appareo), or leather packsaddle is deftly adjusted. This saddle is Mexican, and is considered superior to all others. A tie rope is laid over the saddle rigging, with a 'cinch', or broad canvas band passing under the animal's belly. The test moment has now arrived. The man holding the halter gives himself plenty of jumping room. The packer and his assistant lift a box weighing 100 pounds, and swiftly and deftly lay it on one side of the saddle. There is a flash of tail and heels, a vision of scattering men and dogs, a thud and an atmosphere of dust and emphasizes. When the air clears the box is on the ground, its gaping side protruding cans of compressed beef. The onlookers are

108

several yards removed, the packer is indulging in fine dramatic expression, while the mule, free and untrammelled, is grazing placidly outside the enclosure with only one pricked ear exhibiting any interest whatever in the matter.

By a mingling of endearment and objurgation peculiar to packers and irresistibly funny to the uninitiated Long Ears is once more brought to time. Now he is double blinded and the halter held with a firmer grip. Swiftly and deftly the pack is laid upon him. He snorts, but stands still. A second box is slung upon the opposite side — a wild plunge, a struggle, heels, tail, legs, flying boxes and rapidly moving men. The air doesn't clear this time, the atmosphere is positively oppressive with curdled suppression. Three times the tricky creature baffles them, but the fourth time he submits. The boxes of 100 pounds weight each — he is a young mule and only to be lightly packed on this first trip — are perfectly balanced, the weight coming well to each side and above the shoulders. The rope is adjusted and looped in that noted 'diamond hitch' over the top, the 'cinch' pulled tight with the foot against the animal's side until his belly bulges each side of the broad band; and the work is complete. Long Ears is tied to a convenient tree, not subdued if those ears tell true, but for the time submissive.

The acme of good packing is to enable the animal to carry maximum weight with minimum fatigue and nothing of chafing or discomfort. Durrand of San Francisco, one of the most noted western packers, who is at present helping to pack the Yukon force supplies over the trail, is able to load many of his animals so that they carry 400 pounds yet arrive at the end of their journey in fairly good condition.

A judicious packer who wishes to conserve his working forces will neither overload nor overdrive his animals. But pack-drivers are often indifferent to brutality when away from their employer's oversight, and it makes one's heart ache to see the condition of many animals that return from the trail — pitiful, weary creatures with great angry blotches like inflamed scalds upon their backs, the result of incompetent packing. Sometimes time is allowed for the wound to heal, but pack animals are valuable and pack rates high, and more often the saddles are readjusted, fresh loads put on over the chaffed and broken skin, and the animal walks on in dumb agony, with a festering fist-deep sore fresh goaded every moment by the load above it, until he drops on the trail and is mercifully shot.

It is the animals who suffer most in this. The burden lies heaviest upon the strong, speechless creatures, horses, mules, oxen, dogs — who, side by side with men, break the way into the lonely frozen places of this new land. Perhaps, of all animals, it is hardest to see the oxen suffer. Why we cannot tell, for all are alike dumb in their pain. But horses and mules, even dogs, seem to endure intelligently, as men under protest, or with a knowledge that this is their share in creation's travail of pain, while the oxen look out of the depths of their great brown eyes in such utter bewilderment of the mystery of their suffering that their moans wring one's heart with a passion of pity.

We have already spoken of the fine dogs out here. We got a snapshot yesterday at two plump little fellows, packed all ready for the trail. One carried shot, nails, hammer and tent sets in his bags; the other, their own special food supply, in the shape of dog biscuits and dried meat. Just before starting one of them careered after a squirrel. His troubled master, a foreign looking 'Klondiker', came to our tent door an hour later to make inquires.

"What is his name?" I asked. "Nellie", was the answer. Then, confidentially: "He really is a dog, lady, but we call him "Nellie" because he is so much like a woman in his ways".

Mess call coming at this juncture prevented any further inquiries into the details of "Nellie's"behaviour.

A few days ago one of our party found a dog, a handsome fellow, a mile or two in the bush, watching beside a pair of wornout trousers flung on the ground of a deserted camp. The dog was suffering for lack of food, but refused to leave the relics, which had evidently been cast aside by their owner. Some food was taken to him and he was coaxed at last into a packers camp. He will follow the next pack train and will probably be claimed by some miner far up the trail.

But perhaps the most interesting dog of our journey thus far is "Bush", a pure Alaskan, owned by a tenter here at Telegraph Creek. The pure Alaskan is as rare as the pure Newfoundland animal, and quite as handsome, after his own type. "Bush" is like a wolf transcendentalized, with all the meanness and the savagery left out, and the glory of great benevolence wrought in. He is a little lame in one forepaw, not through any fault of his own, poor brute. He and his consort, an equally handsome fellow, came up the Stikine River in early March, doing brave work in hauling a heavy sledge over the ice. Turned loose at night and enjoying their well-earned rest in the dim light, they were mistaken for wolves by a frightened traveller and shot at. The handsome consort was killed instantly, while "Bush" got the limp in that strong forepaw that will remain with him for life. Our kodak caught 'Bush' on Sunday morning among the preacher's congregation in front of the village store. If he comes

Captain Gardiner, RCD, Faith Fenton and Capt. Bill Robinson of the *Stikine Chief* watch a Klondiker demonstrate his transport

out well the *Globe* will perhaps give his [sic] readers a portrait of the handsomest Alaskan dog on the Stikine River.

One of the elements of strength in our midst, and of pleasure also, is the presence of the Rev. Mr. Pringle, one of the missionaries sent out by the Presbyterian Church for work in the Klondike. He is one of several, we understand. If the others are like him that church is to be congratulated. We speak of him as "In our midst". He is at present stationed at Glenora, twelve miles and a rough up-hill trail away. But that is "in the midst" to this splendid, springy man, who may come swinging up the road any day and hour to take tea or dinner, or a shake-down in camp, have a chat, and then go off again on the return trail, perhaps in time for an evening service, or twenty miles up to see a sick man. He is never weary of step or untimely in speech. He is fearless, outspoken, honest, instant in sympathy, cordial in manner, yet bearing with him always the dignity of his profession. Mr. Pringle is one of those rare men, who, while mixing with all classes of people and giving them unconstrained companionship, yet never permits the flag of Christian manhood to be lowered.

He came up over the Stikine River ice in March. He has lived since then in a wee six feet by eight tent in Glenora. But he is known the district around. He is confidant and friend to all. The miners like him, even when he rebukes, as he does not hesitate to do . The Yukon force like him from the Colonel down to the youngest private. The nurses watch for him as they sit beside their patients far up the trail. His tall, slender, muscular figure is greeted with a shout of welcome as he comes swinging up the hills, his satchel slung over his shoulder, filled with last week's commissions. It is a burdened and bursting satchel when he leaves, for all the 'boys' letters are in it for home, sweethearts and wives. They seem to have faith that their missives will speed more rapidly across the continent when started from this well-liked preacher's hands. It was worth while getting that snapshot on Sunday afternoon, when he sat on a log in the tree shadows, while our boys in twos and threes brought him their letters and commissions. And he took the bursting satchel with its two hundred as cheerily as if it had been a feather-weight, with never a suggestion of that twelve-mile trail and the evening service that was to follow.

Tomorrow he will swing past us with a merry greeting, on his thirty-mile tramp to see a sick private. All honour to such a man!

Messengers come up and down the trail, pausing or entering our camp gates with news. A cheery letter from the Colonel, in advance, of the bush fires fought, the condition of the trail and the nearness of Teslin waters. A request from Captain Bennett's camp, twenty-five miles away, for the doctor. The doctor's orders a day or two later for the nurses, at the base, who strike their tent, and with an orderly behind them go promptly and cheerily down the trail, glad to be of service. It is mountain fever, a form of acute rheumatics, that our poor private has, but the nurses are beside him night and day, and already he is better.* The other members of the Victorian Order nursing staff are on ahead. Thus distributed along the line they are able to be of service and at the call of any detachment. We feel safer and surer because they are with the force. While the occasional applications from sick men outside, shy and doubtful applications, but always cheerily responded to, show the longer need that awaits them.

One more incident suggested by our last topic and our letter is ended:

A tough-looking old fellow, a veritable tramp in threadbare and dust, came into camp one recent day. He wanted medicine and advice from the doctor, Surgeon-Major Foster.

Upon receiving the medicine he asked the price. The doctor hesitated; he has learned not to judge by appearances out here, but this fellow looked an unusual bundle of rags and tags. "Three dollars", he said, doubtfully.

"I haven't any small change about me," answered the patient, producing a handful of bank notes and gold.

"If I had known that I would have charged you five dollars", said the doctor.

"Here you are; we'll call it quits", and the tramp selected his "smallest" — a five-dollar bill.

---

* See Lester diary, 20 June 1898

Teslin, August 28-... Pausing on our march at the moment when we are on one of these ridges of solid ground that rise like high banks out of the swamp, we see on either side of us as far as our vision extends nothing but low lying bog; very far off on our left there are mountains; in the distance on our right there is a swampy lake; but for miles about us and on either side there is only bog of various degrees of stability. Sometimes it is dry and towy [sic], oftener it is wet and spongy, centering in a perfect slough — loam, roadlets, moss and water composite — in which the poor pack mule sinks and is helpless. We are in the very heart of a muskeg country, and as we look about us the doubt arises whether it is possible under any circumstances to make this last thirty or forty miles of trail permanently enduring. The new trail, or new section, to which we have referred, accomplished something, but there is every evidence that many portions of it, if subject to much traffic, will become as soft and impassible as the old route.

If it were possible to find solid ground anywhere in the vicinity a new trail might be made, but one glance over the country from this vantage point shows how hopeless it is in this respect. Besides, there is the curious feature of the country, that this bog is not necessarily confined to the low-lying land, rather it belongs to the hills. It is the soil formation and anywhere, as everywhere, on the hill-tops long stretches of perfectly dry ground are intersected with "soft spots" as the packers term them, or, as we would say in the east, "boggy places".

Surveyors who have studied the ground assert that a good trail can be made over the last forty miles, but only by almost continuous corduroy. A great deal of corduroying has already been done; stretches a good quarter of a mile in length bridge many a soft spot. Yet much remains to be done; there are sections where four and five miles of almost continuous corduroy will be found necessary, and the work will be very expensive.

Yet the important query is whether it can be made enduring. To the eye lacking perhaps technical knowledge there appears to be no solid basis upon which to rest any surface work. This spongy substance has nothing of staying power; it shifts and sways, subject to the action of the ice beneath; and unless the corduroy be built on stilts it appears that the frost and ice of one winter would be sufficient to tear it apart. We saw many instances of inadequate work on our way — corduroy placed early in the season perhaps by inexperienced hands. The bog had worked into deepened holes at either end, the logs had shifted or distended unto desperate packers had flung it [sic] aside and marked it "dangerous" and driven their mules through the 'soft spot' in preference to risking their legs on the obnoxious cordway.

The present men engaged on the trail under the Mackenzie-Mann contract with the British Columbia Government are doing good and substantial work. But looking at all that yet remains to be done, the extent and labour of it, we doubt whether the present season will see the work completed; that is, it is undertaken in any thorough manner. For, let us emphasize it, nothing but costly as well as arduous work will place this last, large section of the Teslin Trail in a permanently good condition.

At the present time of writing, Teslin contains about 200 people, who are living in tents and boat-building as rapidly as possible. There are a few log buildings, a stove containing a small quantity of goods at very large prices, and a liquor establishment, where whiskey retails at $5 per quart . It is only a camping place, and the residence of each camper is made as brief as possible, for the season is late, and every miner and prospector is anxious to get down the lake to their objective winter quarters.

One of the wisest appointments made by the department in connection with the Yukon force was that of Major D.C.F. Bliss, as officer of transportation and supplies. The office has proved both a necessary and responsible one. By its establishment and by the judicious appointment which filled it with an officer so capable, clear-brained and tactful as Major Bliss has proved himself, the department has saved thousands of dollars, and markedly expedited the transport of the supplies.

Upon the earliest possible consultation with the Hudson Bay Company, after the arrival of the Yukon force in British Columbia, it was discovered that only 141 horses had been provided for trans-shipment of the supplies over the Teslin trail. A brief calculation will show the absurd inadequacy of this number. The round trip to Teslin and return takes a pack train nearly one month. A pack train can make only four trips during the season. Each animal averages 200 pounds per pack. Out of the 141 animals, twenty-five must be deducted for saddle horses, packers' food supplies, etc. One hundred and sixteen horses, averaging 200 pounds each carry 33,200 pounds on one trip. In four trips they would transport 132,800 pounds or something less than one quarter of the one hundred tons .

Upon the urgent representations of the commanding officer of the force, Mr. R.H. Hall, manager for the Hudson Bay Company in British Columbia, sent an order for 120 additional animals, 59 of which arrived in Glenora at a later date. The remainder either were not secured or failed to arrive in time to be of service. They may be tied up in the rainy belt or below the canyons of the Stikine River at the present time of writing.

It was at this point that the position and energy of the officer of transport became of value. The Hudson Bay Company, being a big body, moved slowly, very slowly. The transport officer, with 100 tons of supplies at the base of an unknown trail, and September ice and snow rising shadowy at the Teslin end, moved rapidly. For days and weeks, even months, he lived and moved in an atmosphere of pack trains. He scoured the country, and kept an eye upon incoming boats. The tinkle of a mule bell penetrated his deepest reverie, and he was even known to leave instructions with the sentry to rouse him at midnight if, per chance, a boat came in, that he might hasten wharf-ward and be the first to seize upon any four-footed passengers.

It was reported that at a despairing moment he was discovered contemplating the personnel of the force itself with a view of adjusting pack saddles on each.

Seriously speaking, the Major was indefatigable, and his efforts were rewarded by the securement of train after train of animals, until the number which he brought to the Hudson Bay Company [representative], and induced him to engage, doubled those originally secured. These pack trains were owned by professional freighters, and in several instance private parties going over the trail with a small number of animals, packing their own supplies, were glad to make one or more trips for the Government for the sake of the money, while their own stuff waited in caches at wayside camps. The transport officer, in view of the situation, considered it his duty to secure every pack train possible until the transport of the supplies before winter was assured. He made only one exception. No pack train was engaged that had previously promised or contracted in any way with private parties.

This statement is necessary, in view of certain reports that the officers of the Yukon force held inducements of higher rates to secure packers already engaged by incoming miners or prospectors.

Within a month of the arrival of the force in Glenora, several freighters owning large pack trains had been engaged and added to the Hudson Bay stock, the largest of these being the Durrand pack train of one hundred animals, owned by that well-known western packer. These trains, which consisted of animals well broken to the work, made through trips, carrying the necessary food supplies for the advance parties, which, headed by Colonel Evans, were pushing their way up the trail. The 'green' animals — and the Hudson Bay Company's stock consisted largely of these — were packed for short distances along the trail, making relays from depot to depot, thus conserving their energy until that last bad forty miles of muskeg country was reached, when they were in better condition to push through it and reach Teslin without breakdowns.

The fixture of the base at Telegraph Creek was necessarily prolonged by the scarcity of animals, and the fact that the largest trains were making through trips, from which they could not return in less than four weeks, also that every pound of supplies must be sent on the trail before the base could be moved. This being once accomplished, the movement was rapid.

In the meantime the Colonel and his party were at Teslin endeavoring to make the best and most economic arrangements for the transport of the force down the four hundred miles of Teslin Lake and Hootalinqua River to Selkirk. The little steamer *Anglian* of the Canadian Development Company was nearly completed, and after some delay a satisfactory contract was secured for the trans-shipment of the force. Colonel Evans and his party left Teslin on July 20, the *Anglian* contracted to return to Teslin not later than August 25 to carry down the remainder of the force.

The *Anglian*, Teslin Lake

In the meantime, acting under the written instructions of the commanding officer, Major Young, second in command, together with the transport officer, put forth every effort to have full complement of personnel and supplies of the force ready at Teslin on the required date.

Regarding the former there was no difficulty. In the matter of the supplies the situation was more problematic. The Hudson Bay Company, by reason of the contract not specifying any special date of fulfillment, were largely in command of the situation. The transport officer (we speak unofficially and by observation) had been hitherto compelled in all his dealings with the company to use suasion and tactful device, where he should have been able to command. That he possessed these qualities in a marked degree does not condone the situation.

At this point it was clear that the Hudson Bay Company, moving at its then present pace, would not succeed in having the Yukon supplies in Teslin at the date required. Moreover, it lay within the knowledge of the transport officer that a large train of pack mules, recently arrived over the Ashcroft trail, were being employed by the Hudson Bay Co. in their own service over the Dease Lake Trail. Putting suasion aside, and standing within the ground that the Yukon force supplies were not being transported as rapidly as possible, inasmuch as the Hudson Bay Company were not employing all the animals at their command in the Government service, the transport officer impressed these extra animals into immediate service, with the result that every pound of supplies was placed moving up the trail and the last contingent of the force and supplies reached Teslin Lake on August 24, one day earlier than the date fixed for the return of the steamer from Selkirk, and three months from the date of arrival of the force in Glenora. The total number of pack animals employed in packing the Government supplies was something over 500. Of these only 300 had been secured directly by the Hudson Bay Company.

Since the Government contract with the company expired upon the landing of the supplies in Teslin, a summary of the method and conduct of the transport may be permitted from the point of view of an observer. There is no doubt whatever that the Hudson Bay Company, by reason, doubtless, of inefficient management on the part of those officials to whom the supervision was deputed, failed utterly to grasp the necessities of the situation or to make provision for the same. Arguing from the inadequate preparations made and the slow pace of movement, the Yukon supplies would assuredly have failed to reach Teslin Lake in time for trans-shipment down to Selkirk, and would have held a large portion of the force at the former place or at caches along the trail during the entire winter months. That the supplies arrived at Teslin not only previous to the close of navigation, but within five or six weeks of that date, thus giving ample time, in event of the one steamer on the lake not being able to return, for the trans-shipment to Selkirk in scows, is due entirely to the untiring effort and increasing vigilance of the transport officer [Major Bliss], whose service to the department in this connection have been invaluable and deserve highest commendation.

The effect of the passage of so large a quantity of Government supplies over the Teslin trail during the Season has perhaps been unfortunate in so far as it has kept up the packing rates and employed a large number of freighters who would otherwise have been free to pack for civilians, incoming miners and prospectors. But, as previously stated, every care was taken to avoid conflict with the arrangements of civilians, and in every instance where the officers of the force were made aware of such conflict the interest of the civilians was placed first.

The successful trans-shipment of over 100 tons of supplies over the trail in three months, under the circumstances, will certainly prove its possibilities as a trail leading into the very heart of the gold country; for Selkirk and Dawson are not the only objective points to miners coming over the Teslin trail. Nisutlin and Big Salmon Rivers, with all their tributary steams, are being sought and searched. A large prospecting area surrounds Teslin Lake and trail.

To look back over any undertaking and see what might have been done that was not done is one of the privileges belonging to all spheres of human activity: Governments and individuals possess it alike. Had the Militia Department sent an official ahead of the force to confer with the Hudson Bay Co., secure all essential information and make adequate transportation arrangements considerable friction and delay would have been prevented. But that such a company should in any way fall in handling any question of pioneer transport is hardly to be conceived: otherwise doubtless the precaution of sending the transport officer ahead would have been taken.

Viewing the entire situation as it stood upon the arrival of the Yukon force in Glenora, there is no manner of doubt that the commanding officer and his staff have acted in every instance according to the best judgment obtainable and with a view to most expeditious results, namely, that the entire force and its accompanying supplies should not only reach Selkirk by this new and unknown route, but be comfortably housed and stored before the beginning of the long winter season, and their endeavor lies close upon fulfillment.

Georgia Powell's Despatch

Nurse Georgia Powell, who travelled with the advance guard, also wrote a despatch for the Globe *although her story ended at Camp Victoria, on Teslin Lake.*

In camp at Teslin, July 10 - As we are now at the end of our journey, so far as the trail is concerned, I will try to give you a slight idea of our adventures and what we have gone through since leaving Vancouver. We reached Fort Wrangel, Alaska, on May 17, after a very pleasant trip. On Sunday Mr. Sinclair, the Presbyterian clergyman, whom we met at Mr. McLaren's, held services, and on Sunday evening we came into Alert Bay, where we pulled up, and Capt Irving took us to see the totem poles of the Indians. Of course you know what totem poles are, so I am not going to describe this one, but will only say it was thirty feet high and called the finest in existence. There is a store of the Hudson Bay Co. here, and Mr. Hall, one of the managers, being along, he took us to the store and presented us each with a metal bracelet, such as are made by the Indians, as a souvenir. Our next step was at the United States Customs, and the captain took Miss Fenton and me in his boat to the custom house. It is the only house there —dwelling house, customs and post-office. Here the captain put us all in bond.

We reached Wrangel on the evening of the 17th. A big crowd had gathered on the wharf to meet the boat. It was raining, and Wrangel did not look inviting. The Colonel gave orders that the men were not to go ashore that night but after the crowd had somewhat dispersed we ventured forth to see the town. Meantime, Mr. Sinclair had gone ahead and met Mrs. McKinnon, a very brisk and hearty little Scotch woman, who hearing that there were nurses on the ship, came to meet us, and showed us the town in fine fashion. And such a town! Its houses and sidewalks on stilts, for Wrangel is a mudhole of the blackest hue; the sidewalks in such a dilapidated state walking was unsafe; so it was stick in the mud or tumble off in the mud. There are some very comfortable houses, some tents, plenty of saloons, stores and gambling dens in full operation. But, oh, the filth! the sanitary condition anything but good. We saw some very good totem poles, also the remains of the old Russian fort, and spent a very pleasant hour in Mrs. McKinnon's home, by a bright open fire. We stayed on board the *Islander* until all of our freight was off, and left on the 19th for Glenora on the *SS Strathcona*, a boat of the Hudson Bay Co.

We entered the mouth of the Stikine River, eight miles from Wrangel, and then began a most tedious trip against the current, which in this river is very swift and very strong, and it was with much difficulty our boat made her way. The course is very winding and the channel uncertain, the river being so narrow in some places that it seems almost impossible for the boat to make her way through. The scenery at some points was grand, the great glacier, one and a half miles long, [wide] and the grand canyon were sights worth seeing. We sighted the canyon at 3 o'clock one morning and the steward rapped us all up that we might gaze and be filled, and so we did. The wide opening of the mountains, their snowy peaks bathed in the glow of the rosy dawn, made a picture worthy to be gazed on and long to be remembered.

We reached Glenora on the 23rd and camped on a plateau at the foot of a mountain, a mile from the village. Glenora is made up of tents and a few log cabins. There were about 700 people, some of whom were miners waiting to go over the trail, some employed by the MacKenzie & Mann Company on the road, and others who were settled for a time to catch what little they could of the money that was going. We were quite comfortably camped here. Our many bell tents — white in the sun, with the Union Jack waving over all, the many redcoats moving about, the bugle calls echoing through the mountains, all tended to give quite a military air to the little place.

Mr. Pringle, the Presbyterian missionary, and a splendid specimen of true manliness, held service at the camp ground, and the villagers attended. After his morning service at Glenora, this man walked twelve miles over a hard trail to Telegraph Creek, held service there at 3 p.m. and walked back to Glenora and held evening service; three services and a walk of 24 miles every Sunday — what do you think of that for hard work? Good Mr. Pringle! We enjoyed him so much; he often called on us, and many a good story and bit of fun we had, he was so glad to talk to women. His family is in the west. We were two weeks at Glenora.

But I must not forget to tell you how we spent the 24th of May. In the afternoon Col Evans took us all to the village to see the sports and games. There were potato races, sack races, Klondike races, hop, skip and jump — and tug-of-war. The human race was well represented, as there were white men, red men and black men, a big crowd, but a more orderly one I have never seen. Then in the evening the soldiers gave a very good concert, banjo and harp, singing, recitations and speeches, a big bonfire was lighted, a salute fired, we sang "God Save the Queen", and voted that nowhere was her 78th birthday more loyally kept than at Camp Glenora.

We received some mail at Glenora and sent off some, and left there on the 9th of June for Telegraph Creek on the Stikine Creek, twelve miles from Glenora. We were in camp there five days— I say we, for I mean that detachment which is here now; as Col. Evans, with a detachment of 35 men and 30 pack mules, was one day's march ahead of us. Our detachment of 31 men and 30 mules was under command of Major Talbot, Mrs. Starnes, Nurse Scott and myself as incumbrances. The third train has just come in and there are two more to come. With one of these will come the other nurses and Miss Fenton, but when they will reach here is a question. They are not rushing through as we were.

On Sunday before leaving Telegraph Creek a miner came to me and said that he had been sent by "Dandy Jim", the Chief of the Indians, to ask the white squaws if they would attend their services and sing for them. They all wanted to know if we worshipped the same God as they, and, as nurses, how we felt toward the Indian. We went and found quite an assemblage of Indians and their families, some of them very fine looking and intelligent. Mr. Geddes, nephew of Canon Geddes of Hamilton, was reading and

Rev. John Pringle conducting a Sunday service at Telegraph Creek

explaining Scripture to them, in the absence of their missionary, Palgrave. They had never heard white women sing, so we did our best for them in that line, and also talked with them, "Dandy Jim" acting as interpreter.

On leaving Telegraph Creek the trail follows up over quite a high mountain, which was quite a pull on our breath, and a slight foretaste of what was in store for us. The trail is bad, bad for people and very bad for packed animals, all reports to the contrary notwithstanding. From mountain to swamp and bog — bogs into whose cold, damp, mossy depths we would sink to our knees, and under which the ice still remains, swamps where we trampled down bushes and shrubs to make footing for ourselves, and where the mules stick many times, often as many as twenty all down at once, sometimes having to be unpacked to be taken out our baggage dumped in the mud, and where the mosquitoes held high revelry. Let me say right here, for number, size and ferocity these

Much admired by Faith Fenton and Georgia Powell, the Rev. John Pringle of Glenora (left) and his brother George, photographed while serving with the Canadian Expeditionary Force in 1914

mosquitoes cannot be exaggerated, and despite leggings, gloves and the inevitable veil we were badly bitten.

Through the forest we went, where the trail was narrow and the branches of trees threatened our eyes or tore our veils disastrously, through tracts of burnt and blackened country, in some places the ashes still hot from recent burnings, and the dust rising in choking clouds after our feet; through forests of wind-fallen, upturned trees, whose gnarled roots and tangled branches made insecure and often painful footing; over sharp and jagged rocks where slipping would be dangerous, we went trampling, leaping, springing and climbing, a strain that only the strongest and most sinewy women could bear. Our highest mountain climb was an elevation of 1,800 feet in three miles.

We had a horse between the three of us, a stupid, lazy, old pony, whose one ambition was to bang up against every available tree. As I have no patience with laziness in either man or beast, you may be sure I did not take much stock in this horse, but gave up my share to Mrs. Starnes and Nurse Scott. Mrs. Starnes did not ride much. She, being strong, preferred walking to pounding, but I fear Nurse Scott would have been beautifully lean had she walked, though riding was sorely trying. On Sunday, June 10, Mrs. Starnes and I walked seventeen miles. It rained and was cold, and we were drenched and heavy with mud when we made camp at 8:30 p.m., Nurse Scott in little better condition, barring the mud. We always started out ahead of the pack at least two hours. The mules got stuck so often that it would make waiting very dismal for us; besides, the trail was better before they had gone over it.

We used to get up at 2 in the morning, breakfast at 3, tent down and everything packed at 4 and everything on the trail before five. Our lunch, or midday meal, consisted of two hard biscuits and a cup of water from the nearest spring, and I am glad to say good water was plentiful, the only good thing on the trail. Then we had dinner just when the train came in, sometimes 8 or 9, sometimes as late as 11 p.m. Sometimes we would be in camp several hours ahead of the train for we tried to camp where the advance guard did the previous night and as they always left a sign, we knew just where to stop.

One night we made camp about three hours ahead of the train, the mules all being down in the mud, not quite three miles distant from us. We waited and waited till we thought the mules must be all played out, and that the packers had declared to camp where they were. We huddled together on some boughs and I repeated the story of the "Babes in the Woods" by way of comfort and diversion, when some miners who were camped near came to our relief with a bannock baked in a frying pan, some slices of bacon, some evaporated apples, coffee and tea. What mattered it to us that the apples were not sweet, the coffee and tea black? Our hunger sweetened every mouthful and we forgot there was any such thing as butter. We were hungry and thankful accordingly.

Another time we were far ahead of the train, when a man who was in charge of the packing came on to tell us they would camp in the rear, and we would have to go back. Oh dear, the thought of going twice over that piece of trail was surely disheartening, but there was nothing else for it, so back we started. Mrs. Starnes, who was riding, and the man going ahead, Nurse Scott and I following in their track until we came to a swamp, and finding by the print of the horse's feet that they had taken a bye-path to avoid the swamp, we followed on. We had not gone far before we found we were getting out of the direction of the trail, so we retraced our steps back to the swamp, when we thought we heard voices calling to us, and, of course, thought we would better go back again; so, over the little bye-path we went again, and as the calling kept on we answered and went in the direction. The wood was very deep here and we, depending on the calls ahead for our guidance, wandered on, losing all sight of trail and came up to the others only to find that they were more hopelessly lost than we.

The man left us after very strict injunctions to us not to move from the spot, but he came back to us unsuccessful, and as it was growing cold we built a fire. We had quite made up our mind to stay until a rescue party was sent from camp, but you see I am one who cannot remain still when I think something could be done, so I prevailed on the man to allow me to go with him in further search of the trail, as I thought I could remember some landmarks and so together we traced our way by prints in the moss and by fallen trees until we found the true trail. Then I stayed there and kept it, and he went back for the others and we shouted the way back and forth, till we were together again, safe on the homeward trail. You never saw more rejoiced people than Mrs. Starnes and the messenger when they found we were lost, too. 'Misery loves company' is a true saying, and so it proved in this case, for a more miserable couple I never saw, Mrs. Starnes because of being alone and the man from mortification that he had been so misled and brought her into such misery. We made camp at 10:30 p.m. after being lost three hours, and found the rescue party just starting out, but we were none of us so badly frightened that we did not get some amusement and oftentimes fun from our misery and discomfort.

But I think the best fun of all was when we had to ford a river. We had to sit on the horse behind the Major (Talbot), and as the saddle took up a good deal of room and the Major likewise, there was not so much for one to stick on behind, besides our horse objected to extra weight, and as the river was quite deep and the current very strong, the horse plunged and struggled and lost her feet, and it was with much difficulty and frantically hugging the Major that I kept from sliding off into the water. We all had a chance to laugh one at the other, for the sight was too comical, even if the conditions were serious. Then another time the horse thought she would take a bath with Nurse Scott on her back, and so tumbled over into four feet of water. We were rather frightened for a little, but there were three men at hand, who pulled them out wet but unhurt. Again the horse came near drawing [sic] Nurse Scott in the mud, and that was all but a very serious affair for the horse, but beyond a bad twisting and nervous shock she came out unhurt. I had started out with "Victory or Death" for my motto, and the farther on I came the more appropriate I thought it. I wrote it on the many guide posts along as encouragement to those who may come after. We were fourteen days making on, an average a fraction over eleven miles a day.

We met many miners on the route, some returning for supplies and some after packing in their stuff had lost it going down the river and were returning to their homes sadder and poorer men. There are all kinds of trains, horses, mules, oxen, dogs, men wheeling in their supplies in wheelbarrows of rude and weak construction, and men packing in their supplies on their backs, but I think it will be longer ere we see a steam train. When it became known along the trail that there were nurses with soldiers, the miners were all on the watch for us, eager with questions of the world so far behind, or a word of advice of condolence. Fine men they were, some of them educated and refined, for all their uncouth appearance and anxious to show us by conversation and manner that they were not as bad as they might seem. But it is all over now, we say: "It was not so bad after all". We came into camp at Teslin on July 9 and are not sorry to rest. We are as comfortable as we can be under the conditions and rejoice that we have not had so much discomfort from our journey as a cold.

There is not much of a settlement here — a few miners who are building boats to go down the river. The surroundings are rough. Being in the midst of a burnt trail we cannot keep clean or tidy. There are the beginnings of some log cabins, but when the news came that the railroad would not go on the builders gave up, and so a row of roofless log cabins adorn the bank of the river. Across the river the Canadian Developing [sic] Company have a lumber mill and have almost completed a small steamer by which we are hoping we may get passage to Selkirk, for if we wait here to build boats it will take us late in the autumn and there will be barracks to build after that. We are still 400 miles from Fort Selkirk and it may be long before the remainder of the force get here and we may be in Selkirk before they come this far and if the steamer is unable to stem the current up again to get them down, and such fears are entertained, the others will have a long cold wait here, and so the outlook is not very cheerful. Meanwhile, we are trying to stifle our impatience and weary with tent life and its discomforts sigh for the days that are not. I believe arrangements have been made for a weekly mail service between Dawson and surrounding districts and so if it is carried out as it is set forth in the plan we will get mail regularly and safely.

EDWARD LESTER'S DIARY
"UP TO OUR WAISTS IN ICE-COLD WATER"

Wednesday August 17th

The camp [Victoria] which is enclosed by a fence or stockade of logs & brush is situated on a hill overlooking the lake, or rather the estuary of the Teslin river which runs into the south end of the lake.* The guard house & one or two other buildings are constructed of logs as also is the gate-way at the main entrance to the camp. There is quite a settlement here but I have not yet had time to take it in. They are very busy building scows for our transit to Fort Selkirk, of which more anon.** We found only ten or eleven men left here when we got in & the advance party, from their accounts, must have had a terribly hard time getting here. They have all gone to Selkirk by the steamer *Anglian*, the only one on the lake at present & built here for that purpose: she has not yet returned although they are expecting her every day.*** We had a little rain during the night but it is fine today. This is first rain we have had since we cleared the big Hudson Bay summit. We were on fatigue all afternoon, shifting the bacon into the QM stores, & a nice dirty job it was as the hot sun melted the fat & caused it to run out like oil. A party

---

* Today the site of Camp Victoria is marked by a cairn and a plaque recording that it "was erected by the First Battalion, Royal Canadian Regiment on 7 August 1983 to commemorate the long march of the Yukon Field Force and to mark the 100th anniversary of the Regiment."
** "On arrival ... on 30 June steps were at once taken towards the construction of scows and a dock into the Lake — the water near shore being very shallow. On account of the very high charges for lumber asked by the saw mill in operation a saw pit was erected and whip-sawing commenced. A steamboat — the *Anglian* — the property of the Canadian Development Company was almost completed, but the rates asked ($150.00 per passenger and $200.00 per ton freight) to Fort Selkirk, I considered exorbitant, and proceeded with preparations for constructing scows pending arrival of the General Manager of the Company. On his arrival satisfactory rates were arranged i.e. $25.00 per passage and $25.00 per ton weight, with a proviso that in the event of the *Anglian* being unable to return for the remainder of the Force on or before the 25th August, certain scows would be available for purchase from the Company to be used as transport by the Force. Leaving a small party of Artificers to complete the scow and small boat already commenced I proceeded with the Advanced Party per Str. *Anglian* on the 21st July, arriving at Fort Selkirk on the 25th July." — Evans to Adjutant-General, Ottawa, 1 November 1898, in D Hist 73/78.
*** "When the Str. *Anglian* carried the Advance Party from Teslin to Fort Selkirk, in July,

consisting of a Sergt. & three men under Cap. Burstall, together with the "Interior" men started in two small boats for Fort Selkirk. These boats, vary in size from small boats, such as sailed this evening, holding 6 or 8 men & a couple of tons of cargo, to large scows holding 30 or 40 men & a corresponding amount of freight. Capt. Burstall's boat, by the way, carried a lug-sail composed of 4 rubber sheets joined together.

I am not yet certain how long we are to stay here but we shall not move before the 25th, I hear. Sent letter home describing march as far as Fort Evans. I gave it to the lead packer of our mule train to take back to Glenora. Wonder whether it will reach? Doubtful, I should say.

Thursday August 18th

On guard today with Insley & Langille, & Beales (bugler). Corp. Moore in charge. We had a good guard & the guard-room pretty comfortable. It is a log hut, the spaces between the logs being packed or 'chinked' with moss, & the roof is of bark.

A whole tribe of Indians passed the camp this afternoon, shifting quarters. The whole of them, squaws included, carried enormous packs which made what we had to carry look ridiculously small. They were accompanied by the usual allowance of kids & curs.

The weather still continues fine.

Friday August 19th

Coming off guard, consequently had a quiet morning. Some of the Indians who came in yesterday were up in camp selling moccasins & other buckskin articles made by themselves. They were offering some beautifully worked moccasins at $2.50 a pair. I should very much have liked a pair but not having the "needful" had to go without.

Occupied the afternoon washing my clothes worn over the trail I boiled them all afternoon & now they are [still] not clean.

---

the Hootalingua was an easily navigated stream with an ample supply of water. When the *Anglian* returned a month later the water had fallen from three to four feet and she was unable, on account of shallow water, to get further than within 40 miles of Lake Teslin." — Evans to Adjutant-General, Ottawa, 1 November 1898, in DHist 73/78.

After tea a few of us were nailed for fatigue in the Q.M. stores & kept working till after 8 p.m. but I believe we are to get off fatigue tomorrow to make up for it.

The balance of No. 3 Coy. came in today & three pack trains also; they brought mail in with them. I got a letter from Arthur telling me my mother had been seriously ill & not expected to live, but that she was now happily out of all danger & progressing favourably. Latter dated July 10th. They say there is over 100 lbs of newspapers somewhere between here & Glenora but when we shall get them the Lord only knows.

Saturday August 20th

Everyone on fatigue except us who were on fatigue last night. Drs. inspection at 2 p.m.

Sunday August 21st

Church parade at 10.30 p.m. C. of E. service conducted by Capt. Ogilvy; R.C. by Mr. Leduc. Rained a little in the evening but only a slight shower. The Colour-Sergt. is making up [the] number of days working pay coming to each man from Glenora [to] here. I find I am entitled to 18 days. I don't think I mentioned that this is called Camp Victoria.

Monday August 22nd

Raining this morning. Fatigue at QM stores all morning.

Tuesday August 23rd

The last two days have passed uneventfully. We are now doing simply nothing, not even fatigue. We occupy our time eating, sleeping - card playing & boating. There is no sign yet of the *Anglian*. If she does not put in an appearance soon I expect we shall make a start on the boats & scows early next week. Issued with a pair of ankle boots this evening (free issue).

Wednesday August 24th

Major Bliss came in today, also the last pack train, so now all the stores are here.

Thursday August 25th

The weather seems to have broken completely: it is wet, cold, & miserable, but as we have absolutely nothing to do we can stay in the tents all day. I took a walk down the "Town", so called, this evening; at present it contains about 200 who are living mostly in tents & mostly occupied in boat building. There are a few log buildings & quite a pretentious looking store with a veranda in front. This store, by the way, contains a very small quantity of goods at very large prices.

There is also a large colony of Indians here, whose camp we duly inspected. These Indians are rather different to the Indians of the Stikine, who are more or less civilized, but belong to the river & coast tribes, supporting themselves chiefly by fishing. We saw them of all ages & sizes from the new born papoose to one old hag who to judge from her appearance must be a hundred years old. They are, of course, accompanied by the usual allowance of canine monstrosities. They present, however, a very picturesque appearance with their bright coloured blankets striped with all the colours of the rainbow.

I was talking to some fellows camped here who are going on to Dawson. They are all (four of them) Englishmen. One hails from Aldershot, another is a Devonshire man, & a third is an old Owen's College medico. They appear to have had a good many misfortunes but are quite cheerful & jolly over it. One adventure they related was certainly "rough on rats". They had been out after some horses, leaving their camp to look after itself, quite a common proceeding up here where anything left in that way is perfectly safe. They were away all day, being delayed by bush fires, returning at nightfall tired & hungry with visions of a good supper & a comfortable night's rest. Alas for human expectations! When they arrived at their camp they found it had been visited by the fire fiend who had destroyed everything. To add to their miserable plight it came on to rain cats & dogs, so they had to make the best of it for the night with no grub, no tent, no blankets no nothing - that's what I call hard times with a vengeance.

Friday August 26th

We were on fatigue all day getting the stores down to the pier & getting everything ready for loading up the scows. We have rigged up a chute from the top of the hill to the waters' edge, with a carriage carrying about 1200 lbs a load which saves a lot of labour. The carriage is worked by block & tackle. We are to make a start on Monday with twenty days rations. We (the right half-company) go in No. 3 scow with Mr. Leduc.

An extra guard was put on about midnight on account of an attempt being made to raid the stores. Five bags of flour were stolen, four of which were recovered. Suspicions are rife but proof is wanting. It is a significant fact however that flour sells for $20.00 a bag & several men were drunk tonight. The weather continues damp & cold.

Saturday August 27th

Still wet. Fatigue at 8 a.m. Same as yesterday. Issued with oil-skin caps. Half the stores were got on board today. All the rest must be got on board tomorrow.

Sunday August 28th

No Church parade, being busy all day making preparations for start tomorrow. We are to go in our blue fatigue suits taking our oil-skins, with waist belts & pouches & haversacs, no side-arms. All other equipment to be packed in kit bags, except rifles which will be carried on board & then stowed away. Weather showery & chilly. Two large scows, & two somewhat smaller & several small boats, take the whole force. We start at 10 a.m. but of this "I have ma doots".

Monday August 29th

We worked hard this morning getting the remainder of the stores aboard, striking camp, & finally made a start at 10.45 a.m. in the following order. 1st, The flag boat with Major Young flying the [Union] Jack; No. 1 scow, with the ladies, the remnants of No. 1 Coy & the Right Half of No. 2, under Cap. Bennett; No. 2 scow with the Left Half of No. 2 Company, under Color-Sgt. Campbell; No. 3 scow with the Right Half of No. 3

Company, under Mr. Leduc; No. 4 scow with Left Half of No. 3 Coy, under Sgt. Naufts. Caps. Thacker, Ogilvy & Gardiner, with the requisite number of men for crews, were on board the small boats. The boats [scows] have been named as follows: No. 1 "The Lady of the Lake", No. 2 "Bugaboo", No. 3 "La Canadienne", No. 4 "Nova Scotian".

Men of the Field Force test some of the rowboats built from trees they had felled themselves and planks they had whipsawed

The YFF sets sail on Teslin Lake in its home-made scows and rowboats

135

The Log of "La Canadienne"

1st Day

The scow "La Canadienne" is stoutly built & an excellent craft for our purpose, though to the uninitiated she would appear rough & possibly unserviceable. She is a large square-ended scow, roughly built with not a planed board in her & of paint she is as innocent as any young lady of two weeks old. * We started with a fair but light wind. We hoisted our huge lug-sail & with three men working at each of the sweeps we were soon underway. We made about two miles an hour only, & towards noon, when the wind fell, we had a dead calm & we had to labour at the rough-hewn oars, over twelve feet in length & as much as a strong man could lift, with the water still & seeming as heavy as molten lead. Of course we are divided into reliefs for the sweeps. Spence & I manage the sail, Doré & Platt taking turns at the helm. We are the heaviest laden scow of the lot, or at all events we have the most cumbersome cargo, and this interferes with our rowing very much.

Towards evening a brisk breeze sprang up dead aft & we made good headway for a couple of hours, bringing up for the night on a shelving beach, pitching our tents in a low 'bush' near the shore. We built a large camp fire & after having a bit of a chat round it & a song or two we turned in pretty well tired out.

2nd Day - Tuesday August 30th

We made a start soon after 6 a.m. with a fair wind but very light; it gradually died away & soon after noon fell dead calm. Meanwhile, we had got out into the lake which was nowhere more than 2 1/2 miles wide. The shores of the lake slope gradually up to an altitude of perhaps three hundred feet, whilst as a background rise the inevitable, snow-crested, mountains. The beach, which is shelving, is composed of sand &

---

* "The scows were each 46 feet long, 14 feet wide, with a draught of 2 feet when loaded with 15 tons of cargo and about 30 men. Each scow carried 16-foot steering sweeps at bow and stern and two sets of similar propelling oars ranged in the thwarts. Provision was made for a large tarpaulin square-sail to be rigged in the event of favourable winds. For messing purposes each scow was equipped with a sheet-iron stove, fuel and rations." — A.L. Disher, "The Long March of the Yukon Field Force", in *The Beaver* (Autumn 1962), p. 12.

pebbles & there is little or no mud. About noon we sighted a noble group of five mountains rising one behind the other in echelon, as it were, to the height of perhaps four or five thousand feet.

About 1 p.m. a strong breeze sprang up dead against us &, the other scows being lighter than we were, we were soon left far behind. We toiled for two or three hours at the sweeps & did not make half a mile &, the wind increasing, we all had to tie up till the breeze moderated, which it began to do about sundown. We then made a fresh start & went on rowing till dusk.

The sunset this evening was one of the most beautiful it has ever been my luck to see. A deep purple tint clothed the five mountains mentioned above whilst the western heavens displayed every colour of the rainbow, the whole flecked & streaked with crimson & gold, & reflected on the lake which was now calm as a mirror. We pitched our camp on the sandy beach & soon the moon rose &, shining on the still, glassy waters, made a perfect picture for a painter's brush.

Before we turned in the wind, what little there was, turned round to the right quarter so we went to sleep with high hopes for the morrow.

3rd Day - Wednesday August 31st

Strong wind blowing fair down the lake. We made an early start & did not have to touch an oar all day. We could have passed all the scows but tried to keep our proper station. We could not help, however, passing the "Bugaboo" which is frightfully slow. The wind increased so much that we began to have fears for the mast & there was quite a heavy swell. We cracked on, however, & at 5 p.m. brought up for the night having made about 35 miles.

4th Day - Thursday September 1st

Pouring with rain. Made a start at 8 a.m., wind dead against us. Had to row hard all day & only made eight or nine miles at 5 p.m. when we tied up. Pitched camp as usual on the beach. It ceased raining about 6 o'clock but there was still a light air from the wrong direction. If the wind is foul tomorrow we are to lie

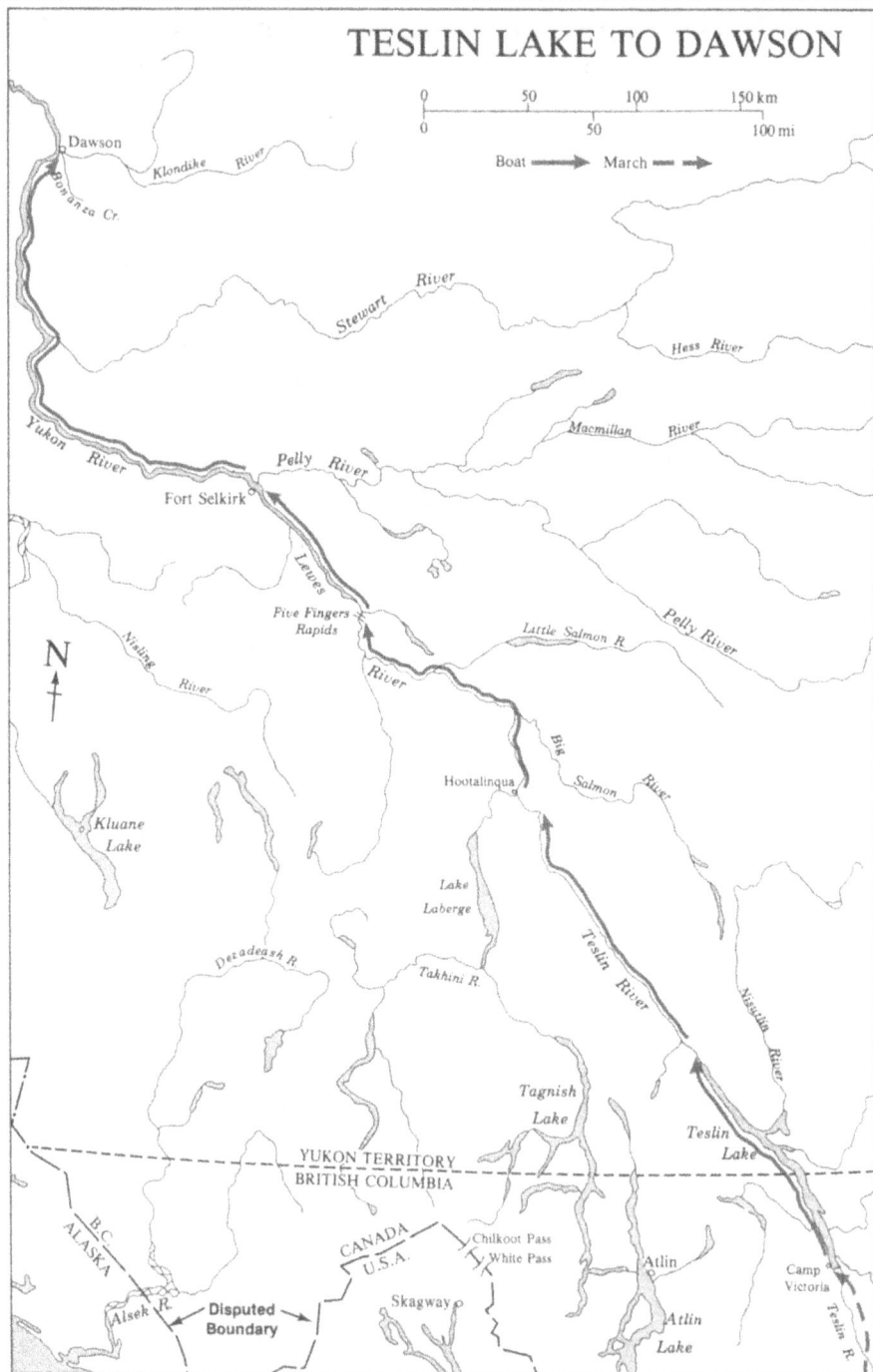

over for a day. We are, I believe, about twenty miles from the mouth of the river which we can just distinguish. We found some wild onions growing here. Some of the fellows have been eating them, but they are very strong & taste earthy.

5th Day - Friday September 2nd

Started off in the usual order at 6.50 a.m. with 21 miles to do. Fine morning with little or no wind. A cross wind soon sprang up & we hoisted our sail to take advantage of it; it was very puffy & we had to keep a watchful eye on our sail. The oars had to be kept going all day & we had a pretty hard day's work. We brought up about 6.45 p.m. right at the mouth of the river. We lie over tomorrow in order to thoroughly overhaul the scows & make some new oars to replace those broken yesterday.

6th Day - Saturday September 3rd

We are lying over today & consequently I am at leisure to write at more length then on the previous five days. It is lucky the powers that be decided not to proceed as there is a regular gale blowing dead against us. We are now lying at the mouth of the Hootalinqua* river, down which we make a start, all being well, tomorrow.

The scenery along the course of the lake has been much the same as that which we have been accustomed to all along the route - snow-capped mountains rising on all sides, clothed with the inevitable spruce forests, mountain torrents dashing down their sides to feed the lake. The water of the lake is most beautifully clear & sweet, the general colour being of a deep blue. In some parts there is a decided swell & I can easily conceive that there is an ugly sea on at times. Just now it is nowhere more than three or four miles wide, but judging from the appearance of the shore it must be several miles wider when the water is high.

---

* At this time the river running *into* Lake Teslin was the Teslin River, and the river running *out of* the lake, linking it to the Yukon, was the Hootalingqua. The latter is now also called the Teslin. The Alaska Highway crosses it at Johnson's Crossing, very close to the site of the Field Force camp of 2/4 September 1898.

Take it altogether, the trip up to now has been a pleasant one though we have had plenty of hard rowing to do. The grub has been decidedly up to the average & we get four meals a day. We bought some moose meat yesterday, from a passing boat, which we are to have for dinner today. The wind is increasing & is now (11 a.m.) blowing very fiercely. We are all short of tobacco & many of the men are using scraped willow bark as a substitute. I have not had to resort to it yet as I have a few pipes' full left but I am afraid I shall have to come to it soon.

Afternoon. I have tasted moose meat for the first time & like it. It tastes very much like tender beef with a slightly sweet taste. There are quantities of cranberries & other berries round the camp the former being particularly plentiful. There are also plenty of partridges, several of which have been brought into camp; if we had shotguns we could get any quantity. I have tried the willow 'tobacco' & although of course not at all like the genuine article it is better than nothing at all (not much). The wind has gone down & the rain ceased & we hope to have a fair wind for our start in the morning. I forgot to mention that we caught several large fish on the lake the names of which I am ignorant of but they run large, fifteen or twenty lbs. We expect to do the trip down the river in eight or ten days.

7th Day - Sunday September 4th

Started off early in the usual order & by 9 a.m. were fairly in the mouth of the river, with a slight current in our favour, with no wind. It is a dull day but up to now there has been no rain. The water is not very deep, the average depth being not much more than four feet [1.1 m]. The banks are well wooded & scenery is very pretty, the foliage beginning to take on autumn tints, a good many poplar & cottonwood trees being mixed with the ubiquitous fir & spruce. The country is now comparatively flat, the mountains standing back & leaving stretches of almost pastoral looking land on either bank, the grass growing in many places luxuriantly, while the woods contain many fine looking pine, spruce, poplar, cottonwood trees.

Here & there the mountains close in on the river & all the way along these mountains are well wooded, & in many places there is a really heavy growth of surprisingly fine trees; & here I should like to remark on the selfishness of some classes of people. Timber is indispensable to the miner & is almost as valuable as the gold itself, & yet so thoughtless & indifferent are these people that for hundreds of miles along the river & lake, & in fact along the whole trail, the woods may be seen ablaze, ignited from camp fires carelessly left burning. These hundreds of square miles of excellent timber must have been destroyed through the selfish indifference of men who would not stretch out a hand for a pail of water to save from destruction millions of cords of wood which did not belong to them. Timber is already scarce & a few more years of this sort of work will inevitably result in a timber famine & then goodbye to the Klondike mining industry.

10 a.m. We are now passing between high banks of yellow clay or sand & the current is increasing in swiftness so that we only have to keep the scow straight. The wind is also fair & just strong enough to ripple the water, the sun is shining brightly, so it is very pleasant although there is a sharpness in the air which makes it advisable to keep a coat on. At noon we passed through a small rapid which we shot at the rate of about ten miles an hour & soon after passing this we struck on a sand bar swinging completely round twice & then getting clear. This river, which is called the Hootalinqua, is a fine stream about a mile in width, with beautifully clear water. It swarms with fish & the small boats have been hauling them up, hand over fist. It abounds with sand bars & shoals & we have to feel every foot of our way.* We made about 35 miles & camped in a very pleasant place. The tents are pitched on some long swamp grass but in front of them is a perfect quagmire. We had moose meat for dinner & fish for tea. The fish, of which I have no idea of the name, the flesh of which is a bright yellow colour, was the most delicious flavour I have tasted.

* "Oh! the joy of just drifting near the shore and seeing the shadows and the fearless ducklings come quite near us. The Major [Young] stopped the men from shooting game, for it got us out of formation. The river ran about 8 miles per hour, wearing the shore in one place and piling it up in another. Even with the greatest care we often got on a sandbar. The men wore high gum boots. Captain Bennett was just from the military school in Halifax and full of fun and nonsense. About 4 p.m. the scout would look for a camping spot for the night: then by the bugle call we'd know on which side of the river to land." — "Rachael Hanna's Diary," *loc. cit.*

It keeps fine & has every appearance of a fine day tomorrow. There are plenty of bear tracks on the shore near the camp but we have not yet caught sight of one: wild fowl however are very plentiful though very hard to get with a rifle, still several ducks have been shot.

8th Day - Monday September 5th

Reveille at 5 a.m. instead of 4.30. We were all ready to start by 6.30 but were unable to get away before 8.15 on account of the mist on the river. At last however the fog lifted, the sun came out & we started out with every promise of a glorious day. About 10 o'clock we passed three large scows laden with cattle, bound for Dawson. At 1 p.m. the day was gloriously fine & we were passing between high cliffs of sand crowned with foliage of all colours, in fact, this part of the river is very beautiful. The current is very swift, & here & there we met with rapids which required all our skill to navigate.

Soon again, as yesterday, the mountains close in on the river on each side, rising up sheer from the river's edge & wooded up to the very summits. About 5 p.m. the "Bugaboo" got aground on a sand bank & we all had to heave-to & wait for her. By the time she got up it was too late to proceed, so we camped for the night having made about 35 miles. Just before this we passed a light raft laden with sheep. She was hard & fast & the crew were busy unloading her to get her off.

9th Day - Tuesday September 6th

There was no fog this morning & we got off soon after 7 a.m. The current was getting swifter all the while & we slipped along at a good pace. All scows touched here & there but all went well till about 2 p.m. when we passed the "Bugaboo", aground, & immediately afterwards struck heavily ourselves, swung broadside onto a shoal, & there stuck. Then the fun began; all hands had to tumble overboard, up to our waists in ice-cold water, & pull & haul for about twenty minutes, till at last we swung clear & went on our way, damp but rejoicing.

We passed two camps where gold washing was going on but were too far off to make any inquiries. All went serene for the rest of the day till just before we stopped for the night, when we struck on a sunken rock & all but capsized. We swung clear, however, sustaining no damage as far as we could make out. We have made good distance today and are now under 200 miles from our destination.

10th Day - Wednesday September 7th

Morning fine but rather chilly at first. Made a start at 7.30 a.m. The first ten or twelve miles was very good going & free from rapids and sand banks. Grand scenery, beautiful with autumnal tints. Water rather thick, looks as if there had been rain somewhat upstream. There is a post of the N.W.M.P. some thirty miles or so down, which we hope to make tonight. We had no mishaps today, with the exception of just touching now & again.

At 4.30 p.m. we passed the junction with the Thirty Mile River, at which there is a small settlement called Hootalinqua & a post of the N.W.M.P. mentioned above, & where we saw a small stern-wheel [paddle] steamer lying. This Thirty Mile River is where the Skagway route joins this, & when we passed a large scow was just coming down. We went on about fifteen miles further & then camped for the night having done nearly fifty miles today. The river we are now descending is known as the Lewes; * it is much wider & deeper & very swift. The water has the peculiar greenish tint of the Tahltan & Nahlin, being mostly glacial & icy cold.

11th Day - Thursday September 8th

Dense fog this morning which prevented us making a start before 8 a.m., by which time, however, it had cleared completely away & we went bowling merrily along under a cloudless sky & a bright sun. The current carried us along at the rate of about five or six miles an hour & up to noon we had no shoals or sand bars to trouble us. The scenery was grand & the whole thing up to now has been nothing more nor less than a huge pleasure trip & I for one shall be quite sorry when we reach Ft. Selkirk,

---

* The Thirtymile and Lewes rivers of 1898 are now the upper Yukon.

always providing the weather keeps fine. The only thing we find hard is the scarcity of tobacco, in fact I don't believe there is half a pound amongst the whole crowd. I heard $5.00 offered & refused last night for a single plug of 'T&B'. I myself offered $2.00 for one without success two days ago.

We made over fifty miles today without mishap & are now about 115 miles from Ft. Selkirk — which we hope to reach by Saturday morning at the latest. We shall probably strike the 'Five Fingers' rapids on Saturday. These are said to be the most ticklish part of the journey & will require careful navigation to get through without disaster. We passed the junction with the Big Salmon river about 2 p.m., with a Mounted Police station. The police barracks are prettily situated amongst the trees. The log buildings are not particularly pretentious but they look comfortable enough to us who have been under canvas for so long, & they doubtless serve their purpose well. Here the police compel everybody to land (of course we were exempt) & have their goods inspected to prevent whiskey smuggling.

12th Day - Friday September 9th

Pulled out about 8 a.m. Fine weather & a swift current. We had no mishaps & did a good forty miles, passing the mouth of the Little Salmon river about noon. There are a couple of police stationed there who were seated on the bank as we passed. We lay for the night some seven or eight miles from 'Five Fingers'. During our stay here, I think it was about 8.30 p.m., two steamers passed down, en route for Dawson.* They were a pretty sight with all their lights showing up against their black hulls.

13th Day - Saturday September 10th

It was 8.15 p.m. before we made a start under the usual cloudless sky & all went well till about 10.45 when we caught sight of the much talked-of Five Finger Rapids which we shot in fine style, through the right of the five channels through which the river rushes, a boiling torrent between high rocks. We

---

* These would have come from Lake Bennett, bringing goods and passengers from the Skagway/White Pass route.

experienced no difficulty at all & there seemed to me to be very little danger.* A few miles further on we passed the 'Rink Rapids' which were of still less importance, always providing you take the right channel. The right channel is the right in both senses of the word & we heard of no accident to anyone who took this course.

The dangers of these rapids have been much overrated & apropos of this, "taking one consideration with another" I have been forced to the conclusion, both during this part of the journey & on the trail, that either the people who wrote about the trail were grossly ignorant regarding its conditions or they were affected with a complaint of which the most characteristic symptom is an unparalleled love of exaggeration & misrepresentation. In some parts of the world people so affected are called "liar", sometimes coupled with one adjective, more or less gaudy. But in this part of the world the practice is so common that the failing is looked upon as a natural mode of expression. We noticed it again & again on the march, especially with regard to distances & the condition of the trail.

Soon after passing the Rink Rapids the river widens & is dotted all over with islands so that the Scout [row] boats were puzzled to find the right channel & it was practically impossible to avoid touching bottom now & then. At 3.30 p.m. we met a large steamer, the *Columbian*, pretty well crowded with passengers amongst whom we recognized Major Talbot.** All went

---

* "... turning suddenly to the right a great barrier looms up a mile ahead — five great irregular blocks of reddish rock ranging across the river like the piers of a bridge — making two principal channels. That on the left is growling ominously over shallow rocks, so we turn to the right and drop into a small eddy a few hundred feet above the great wall. We climb up and look at the rapid. It seems by no means dangerous. The opening is about one hundred feet wide, with vertical walls, through which the river suddenly drops a couple of feet, the waves rising angrily in a return curl, then dancing on in rapidly diminishing chops until lost in the swift current below. ... Without waiting we turn our prow squarely for the middle of the cleft; a drop, a smash, a few quarts of water over the sides, and we are shot through into the fast current, without even looking back." — E.T. Adney, *The Klondike Stampede of 1897-1898* (New York, 1900), pp. 156-7.

** Talbot was on his way back East, having been granted two months' leave by Evans "on account of the sickness of his wife". The GOC Militia recommended to his Minister that Talbot's appointment to the Field Force be cancelled as his reason was "an insufficient one". This was an internal disciplinary matter that normally would not concern the Minister, but "I bring it, however, to your notice as the composition of the Yukon Field Force was, I understand, originated by you". Subsequently Evans assigned special praise to Talbot for his work

well till about 5 p.m. when we were going gaily on our way & I am afraid not paying much attention to our course. In fact, we were all engaged in an animated & noisy argument concerning a large animal we could see on the hillside, some declaring it was a moose, whilst others contended it was nothing more or less than an old horse; the dispute ran high when suddenly bump! Crash!! We were hard & fast on a sand bar.

The Five Fingers rapids on the Yukon river

All thoughts of the moose vanished. Loud & deep were the imprecations poured upon the head of that inoffensive animal, whatever it was, as all hands tumbled overboard in the icy water, & push & haul for ten or fifteen minutes to get the scow off. We succeeded at last but I noticed that the discussion appeared to have lost much of its former warmth. Soon after this incident we hauled in for the night only ten or fifteen miles from Selkirk. There was a very fine exhibition of the Northern Lights, tonight's far exceeding in brilliancy all I have ever seen.

during the march into the Yukon and reported that he had carried important despatches back to Ottawa with him: Talbot was permitted to return when his leave expired (GOC to MMD, 6 October 1898 and DOC MD 7 to OC 8th Battalion, 19 November 1898, in PAC, RG 9 II, B 1 Vol. 280 ff 77013) but, in fact, chose to retire rather than return and was not replaced.

14th & Last Day - Sunday September 11th

At last we have finished our long journey & are safe & sound in port at the long talked-of Fort Selkirk.* We arrived here at 1.30 p.m. after a somewhat eventful journey. The river widened out very much after we left our last night's camping ground, & is studded all over with islands forming innumerable channels which made navigation very difficult. We got aground several times & once got hard & fast with the usual result - all overboard. It took us half an hour to get off this time & this, of course, threw us a long way behind; the other scows, however, [also] kept sticking & this enabled us to catch up & so reach Ft. Selkirk in our proper position.

There was mail awaiting us when we arrived & I got some newspapers, in one which I found the Swedish knife I wrote home for. I am dead tired so will write no more tonight but will leave description of camp here till a more favourable opportunity.

Faith Fenton and photographer H. J. Woodside rest during the long march over the Teslin Trail.

---

* A year earlier, shortly after Ottawa had decided that the territorial capital should be there, E.T. Adney "finally drew up in front of a cluster of log buildings where a trodden path leads up the snow-covered bank.... . The site of the old post is still pointed out, a few yards in the rear of the present buildings, which consist of a store and dwelling-house built of logs and several log-cabins, belonging to Arthur Harper, an agent of the Alaska Commercial Company. These buildings, and some others in the distance, occupied by Indians, and a mission, and along pile of cordwood, are all that meet the eye..." — Adney, *loc. cit.*, pp 158-161.

FAITH FENTON'S LAST DESPATCH
"THE YUKON JOLLIES"

Dawson City, Sept. 21 - They made quite an imposing appearance as they lay at the small wharf down below the camp hill - four scows and five small boats, all yellow and piney with the newness of fresh cut lumber. "The fleet" we termed it in the magnificence of camp parlance, and "the fleet" it remained throughout our long water trip, albeit surely the most unique one that ever sailed high seas or inland waters.

The little steamer *Anglian*, the only one on the lake, which had carried our advance party down to Selkirk four weeks earlier, was to be granted three days' grace beyond her return date, Aug. 25 — so ran the Colonel's orders — and if she failed to arrive, the main body of the Yukon force, now all assembled at Teslin, were to load the scows with the remaining supplies, man the fleet and, under the command of Major Young, set sail for our long delayed and final port — Fort Selkirk.

The 25th came and passed without sign of the little steamer: another day and yet another, and the morning of the third found the men busy loading the scows, so that not an hour's delay should intervene. When night fell everything was ready: the order of our going and the regulations to govern the voyage were duly read out and impressed by an anxious Major upon the junior officers, who were disposed to view the trip in frolicsome light; and when the sunny morning of the fourth day broke it was "tent struck and away" on this last stage of our summerlong journey.

Was there ever a more unique spectacle than our fleet presented as it moved out from the little camp wharf? Could it have sailed in such fashion up the teeming Thames how the London sailor world would have stared and laughed, then cheered itself hoarse for its colonial comrades-pioneer.

First came three small boats ranged at successive distances, the scout, Capt. Thacker, and his oarmen well in advance; Major Young, the commanding officer, second, and the despatch boat for general service third. These were followed by the four scows, each about one hundred yards apart., while two small boats containing doctor and quartermaster brought up the rear. The fleet, when in motion, covered over half a mile. The scows and boats were of tough, unpainted pine, yet damp from the sawmill. The former were strongly put together, fitted with pumps, rude rudders and immense oars. They averaged loads ranging from ten to thirteen tons each and carried about thirty men. Great sails of tarpaulin helped them down the lake. Each carried for mess purposes two of those absurd yet useful travesties, the sheet-iron camp stove, and each was thronged with merry soldier boys in yellow sou-westers, fatigue suits frayed by the trail, and every variety of footgear. The commander's boat carried the flag and the bugle, and these, with the occasional scarlet coat among the men, gave the military touch and acknowledgement.

Gaily they put out from Teslin, headed by the little boat with the well-loved colors dipping from its bow; gaily the bugle rang out its command, and gaily the yellow hatted fellows tugged at the giant oars, while the stovepipes puffed cheerily and the cooks with bared arms and prodding forks hovered over the stoves perched amidships or at the stern.

A fleet of Chinese junks might bear some resemblance, but possibly the camping miners on the bank expressed the inexpressible by the shouted inquiry, "Say, you fellows, where in the devil's name did you come from and what are you anyway?"

"Soldiers," "Marines," "Klondikers," "H.M.S. the Yukon Squadron," the replies rang back with laughter, but the man who knew his Kipling was ready:

"Now there isn't no room to say ye don't know -
They have proved it plain and true -
That whether it's Widow, or whether it's Ship.
Victorier's work is to do:
And they done it, the Jollies - Her Majesty's Jollies -
Soldier and sailor, too."

And they certainly did it - our Yukon Jollies - with a right good will, on our long four hundred mile scow journey down

A Dawson street scene

The 'tent city' raised along the Dawson flats by eager Klondikers, 1898

Group taken at midnight at the Yukon police barracks-June 1899. L to R: Supt. S.B. Steele (NWMP), Miss Scott, Insp. C. Starnes (NWMP) and Mrs. Starnes, Capt. Burstall (Yukon Field Force) later Major General Sir Harry Burstall (Chief of General Staff)

unknown lake and river, through shoals and eddies, currents and rapids, to the golden Canadian Northland.

It is impossible within the limits of one article to speak in detail of this unique trip; and it is doubtful whether the daily incidents of laughter and lunch, discomfort or mishap, night camp and morning start, would be of interest to the public at large. These things will remain valued memories only to those who shared the voyage together. Here it is ours rather to give an impressionist sketch of the trip together, with whatever of fact may have woven itself by observation into our journey.

Looking back from this vantage point, or disadvantage point, of Dawson City, a week after our arrival, the voyage resolves itself into thirteen days of rapid gliding down as fair a waterway as any of eastern Canada can show. First Teslin Lake, some sixty miles long; then the Hootalinqua, about 140 miles, slipping from it imperceptibly into the Lewis [sic] River for nearly 200 miles and from that again into the Yukon. It is all one river and one waterway from Teslin Lake down; the changing names are a confusion and mistake. It is a splendid, clear sweep of five hundred and fifty miles course, between grand banks and low-reaching mountains. It is one of Canada's superb rivers — fairer than the Saguenay and swifter than the great St. Lawrence, yet bearing to this far Yukon land the same vast waterway connection that the latter does in eastern Canada. It is second only to its big brother stream, the Mackenzie. Yet this river — Teslin, Hootalinqua, Lewis, Pelly, Yukon, or what you will, for the last name is inclusive of all the ramifications — is greater than all, inasmuch as its sands are golden, its hillsides and benches rich with yellow quartz.

Believing that all mountain rivers resemble each other largely, we had looked for a second Stikine, shallow, rushing and full of snags and shoals, but this splendid, swift-flowing stream opened its vista of miles before us with an every increasing surprise. Throughout its entire distance above Selkirk the river is never very wide. Teslin Lake, which is but a river expansion, although sixty miles long, rarely passes beyond three miles in width, usually less than a mile. The river varies from fifty yards in the earlier portion to two hundred yards as it nears Selkirk.

Teslin Lake is literally a lake among mountains — they encompass it entirely. It is here, perhaps, that the scenery is finest — not in any bald, frozen fashion, but in a beauty of low and distant mountain peaks, pushed back from the shore by shelving sandy beaches and dwarfed pine bushes.

On our second evening out we camped on such a beach some thirty miles down the lake. It was the banner night of beauty in all our two weeks' journey. The day had been one of splendid warmth and sunshine. The fleet, by hard rowing against a head wind, had made fifteen miles, when at 6 o'clock the bugle sounded the halt. Scow after scow turned shoreward, and dislodged its load of merry men. Tents were pitched, and the evening meal served, the men moving about in a glory of sunset color, not glowing with crimson, as in the east, but full of exquisite purples and browns. From deepest velvety purple, through shades of violet and hellotrope, to delicate pearly grey, the higher mountains stood like richly mantled kings, while the lower hills, pine green to the timber line, caught the sun upon their bald, moss-covered brows in a harmony of browns. The lake stretched its half-mile of blue from bank to bank, while far off between the lower heights three snow-capped peaks caught the one touch of scarlet. It might have been Norway, but nothing was hard or violent, for a gentle warmth was in the air, and a cobweb breeze toned to delicate softness. Only a Canadian northland sunset — but the most perfect and richest bit of color I have ever seen.

Come up to the Yukon, O artists of our country! You who have such rare delicacy of touch for landscape light and shade, and by your gifted pencils let our people know the rare summer beauties of this much-mailigned land —our artistic Norway, our Switzerland — yet fairer than these — our beautiful northern Canada!

It is not our intention to convey the impression that the entire trip was easy sailing in deep water. We came aground on shoals at various points, but it was from lack of knowledge of the correct channel. Our own observation and experience lead us to coincide with Mr. Ogilvie, who in his report on these rivers says repeatedly that he had no doubt that at every point a good channel can be found. Teslin Lake and River have not yet been charted; our fleet navigated pioneer water in this respect. Without question, to bring these heavily laden scows, drawing nearly two feet, down such a length of unknown waters, with only the certainty that at some points somewhere there were shoals and rapids to encounter, was a responsible undertaking. That it was accomplished in safety is a matter of congratulation to Major Young and the men who worked so heartily under his command.

Our sail down the lake, a matter of five days, between head winds and oars, was free from mishap, or excitement; the fun began on our second day after entering the river. The current runs about two miles an hour at the start, increasing rapidly to three and four miles, reaching at one point from five to seven miles speed, and decreasing again as we near Selkirk to about three or four miles, which it maintains to Dawson. The river is fairly straight for the first thirty miles after that it takes a series of sharp turns, and for the next hundred miles curves and doubles in a manner worthy of the shallow Stikine, but there are no snags, and the shoals lie chiefly within a sixty mile range on the upper portion of the river.

On our second day, after, passing through a picturesque canyon, our fleet entered upon a series of 'riffles' as they are termed here, or small rapids that continued throughout two days voyaging and kept the rowers lively. The scout boat would shout back regrading the channel, the bugle ring out the signal "right", "left" or "centre"; but the current was swift, and frequently the call came too late for the cumbersome barges. One or another would run on the outstretched shoal and swing helplessly broadside or stern down stream. "Overboard, men" the young scow captain would say, and in an instant every man would be waist deep in the rushing water, pushing with a "heave-oh-heave" until the bulky creature swung off, and the dripping fellows clambered cheering aboard, to be quenched by the anxious steersman's shout as the barge swept into a fresh rapid: "Confound you, stop cheering and port — port like the devil."

In and out between the shoals, over the riffles, and around perilously sharp-turned banks, carried on by the current, yet with always a channel, did we but know it, the scow fleet sped through two splendid days. The rear scows, profiting by the mishaps of No. 1, would often find a safer channel. Sometimes the scout's warning came too late, and barge after barge would run aground. At one moment on the trip two, three and four were all lodged on a hidden bar and swinging bow and stern, while No. 1, who had escaped looked back in triumph as they sped on with the current. But the commander's regulations required a tie-up for the free scows in such instance until all hove in sight and resumed their distances.

It was a journey among the wilds for the first two hundred miles, with little sign of life or habitation upon the banks, but as we neared the Thirty-mile, or Lewis river junction we caught our first glimpses of the gold quest. Here was a "claim" staked out on the bank, with a few poplar boughs marking the water boundary. Here was a 'cradle' lying idle, and here a sluice box. Camps grew frequent, while picturesque fellows in bright-colored jerseys shouted salutations and queries from the banks.

Just below the river confluence of Lewis and Hootalinqua (or Teslin) Rivers we passed the famous Cassiar bar, a low-lying stretch of sand, every bit of which is "staked". It was from this bar that so much gold was taken a year or two ago. It gave us the first full conception of the fascination, the simplicity and the gambling of gold mining — only a low-lying bit of sand, half covered with stunted shrubs, such as might be passed by the score on any river; yet it has yielded hundreds of thousands [of dollars] in yellow dust. It is primitive still — only numerous tents and 'stakes' with sluices and 'cradles' here and there on the low bank proclaim its possibilities.

There are but two marked scenic points between the river confluence and Selkirk — the first, 'Eagle's Nest,' an abrupt rock mountain of light grey stone, about 500 feet in height. Since the bluff banks of the river throughout the entire distance are of pure clay formation, this mass of stone stands out as a peculiar feature. Then there are the Five Finger Rapids — five masses of rock standing across the river, as Percé Rock stands out to the Atlantic sea, with the stream flowing in turbulent rapids between each. There is one navigable channel close to the right bank. It is only some forty feet wide, and a sudden curve in the river just above makes it difficult to get into the channel centre. If a large boat misses the centre by a few feet it would be forced on by the current and crashed against the granite rock wall on either side.

The odds were great, with bulky, slow-steering scows, and the Major's jolly face grew grave as, drawing his little boat to shore just above the rapids, he looked up at the oncoming scows with their burden of men. They were at a point where no word of his could avail. Down sped No. 1 striking the channel centre exactly. We could almost touch the frowning rock as we sped through the turbulent tossing narrows. Down came No. 2 and No.1 looked back to cheer. Would No. 3 strike it? She had turned a little; she was out of the current; would she right herself in time? The Major grew white. "God help the poor fellows if she misses," he muttered. Ah! she has cleared it and down she speeds in safety, with No. 4 close following.

After that came fifty miles of easy sailing among bars and small islands and thus we came to Selkirk, where within an hour we caught a passing steamer and continued on to Dawson City.

Of the superb weather we have spoken only incidentally. In view of the conception that has been given to eastern Canada of perpetual ice and snow and blizzard bitterness, it seemed impossible that we should experience such fair September days. Toronto could have given us nothing finer than these early September weeks of voyage down the Yukon. Warm even to heat, sunny and gentle of breeze, with evenings fast drawing into darkness, yet not too cold for the nightly tent-pitching and camp fire. Just such days and nights as our Ontario September gives us. Yet we were voyaging down the Yukon and travelling in the sub-arctic.

To-night — September 21 — I write in a small tent snugly placed within a corner of the Mounted Police barracks. It has a flooring, and my little stove burns brightly, it is true, yet I find it as comfortable and habitable as any September tenting would be in the east.

The transition from summer to winter is very abrupt, they tell me, and snow may come to-morrow. It may be so, yet I speak only from experience in asserting that thus far excepting the frequent, almost general, fall in temperature at night and exceptional days, there has been little difference between this Yukon summer and any one of our cooler summers in eastern Canada, and it has been a summer extending from late May to mid-September.

It seems at this point a fitting thing to write a few brief farewell words concerning the Yukon force in its personnel, our comrades in a long and fair summer journey, whom we left at Selkirk. The men are good fellows every one. On trail, on scow, in road-making or barrack-building they were 'ready, aye, ready,' for pioneer work in all its variety.

Their Colonel is thoughtful for them and proud of them, and they are ready to yield him all respect and honor. We write thus in recognition of the absurdly exaggerated report concerning disaffection and mutiny in the force that some chance eastern papers of early summer brought up to us over the trail. The report was credited to members of the Interior Department travelling with the party. They came to your correspondent indignantly denying the charge and requesting the publication of their denial. A private was dismissed from the force at Glenora for insubordination, and this incident was the foundation of the report. The slight nature of the trouble may be inferred from the fact that your correspondent, in common with many members of the force and its attaches, was unaware of the occurrence until papers containing double-column, sensational articles with their flaring headings found their wandering way up the trail and elicited inquiry.

For the courtesies extended to the small group of women under their care we make instant and cordial acknowledgment both to officers and privates. Among both there are men whom each of their feminine comrades of a season will be proud to rank as friends.

EDWARD LESTER'S DIARY
LIFE AT FORT SELKIRK

Having arrived at Fort Selkirk, there was still much work for the Field Force to do before winter set in. The advance party had already constructed the essential buildings, but stores had to be moved up from the river and organized in a convenient fashion, fuel had to be cut, hauled, sawn and stacked, and the fort generally put into condition to keep its garrison snug through a Yukon winter.

Monday September 12th

Yesterday we pitched camp as usual, as although the barracks are well on their way towards their completion they are not yet fit for occupation. We were all on fatigue at 8 a.m., unloading the scows and getting the cargoes up to the QM stores. We worked till past dinner time in order to finish and were allowed the afternoon to ourselves. We got some tobacco but had to pay $1.00 per plug for it. I hope we shall soon get our own supplies or I, for one, shall have serious thoughts of joining the Anti-Tobacco League.

Tuesday September 13th

Working parties were formed today. We did ten solid hours today, viz. 7 a.m. till 12 noon, one hour for dinner, then 1 to 6 p.m. Of course we are on working pay. * This is to continue till the barracks are completed. The weather is now getting very cold and we shall be very pleased to get into our winter quarters as the tents are anything but warm at night. The huts, we hope, will be finished by the end of this week or the beginning of next.

Our job today was cutting and bringing in logs and building a rack to hang the bacon on. After finishing this we started washing and scraping and washing the bacon which had got covered with all kinds of filth coming over the trail; after this we brought it up & hung it on the racks. We got through about half & shall be on the

---

* "Working pay" brought the men receiving it an extra 40 cents a day, in addition to the double pay that all members of the Force were entitled to, making a total of $1.20 *per diem* for a private soldier

same job tomorrow. There are about a dozen of us on this job. The others are all busy, some gathering moss [to chink the logs of the buildings], some employed on the buildings, etc.

Fort Selkirk before the barracks were built.

Wednesday September 14th

Finished our bacon job, having scraped, washed, & hung over 500 sides. I am unable to write much these days as I am always dead tired. * By the time supper is over I am quite ready to roost. It is quite dark now by 7:30 p.m. & there is sharp frost every night. The Colonel has gone to Dawson to see about our winter supplies, none of which have arrived yet. The nurses and Miss Fenton have also gone. ** We expect the Colonel back every day.

Thursday September 15th

Another hard day's work got through. We have been hauling

---

* In the "heavy and dangerous work of logging and rafting on the cold and rapid waters of the Yukon, and afterwards in the construction of Fort Selkirk, entailing as it did ten hours steady labour daily", Colonel Evans considered that "the soldiers more than set the pace for the civilians employed at the same work at far higher rates of pay" — D Hist 73/78.

** Faith Fenton would not be the first female correspondent to reach the Klondike, however. Flora Shaw of the London *Times* (later Lady Lugard, wife of Britain's West African pro-

Building the barracks at Fort Selkirk.

logs from the river & getting them ready for sawing up into cordwood. There was a steamer up from Dawson this afternoon but she brought nothing for us. We are terribly tormented by a species of small black fly of which there are millions; they are worse than the mosquitoes & more venomous. The weather keeps fine & is quite warm during the day but very cold at night & it is rather uncomfortable in the tents.

Friday September 16th

We were on the same job today, viz. hauling & sawing logs. A large steamer, the *Columbian*, passed down but brought no mail. The day has been fine but just before we knocked off for the night a violent gale arose, causing the burning rubbish heaps to spread

---

consul) arrived in the Klondike via Skagway and the White Pass on 19 July. At the Mounted Police barracks in Dawson, Fenton set down a pet cat she had brought all the way from Vancouver. Police huskies promptly tore it to pieces before anyone could intervene.

A winter parade of the Field Force. Note the Maxim gun (and the dog) at the rear.

rapidly in the direction of the new buildings. All hands were soon fighting the flames to save the buildings which, at one time, were in great danger. After about an hour's hard work we got it under control & soon after a heavy rain completed what we had commenced. It is now 8 p.m. & the rain is descending in torrents.

Saturday September 17th

The rain continued to pour down till about 10 o'clock last night when it cleared & commenced to freeze hard, & our tent this morning would have stood without the pole. We worked at logging all the morning & then knocked off for the day as we fondly hoped,but, alas, our hopes were dashed to the ground as first there was Dr.'s inspection, then inspection of arms, after which a steamer came in with some heavy goods from Dawson which we had to lug from the wharf, a distance of about a quarter of a mile. The goods consisted of box-stoves, kegs of nails, & after this we were actually free!!!

There is a Church parade tomorrow & then, bar accidents, the day to ourselves. No. 1 Coy., in the advance party, who were camped about 1/2 a mile lower down, moved up today & went into No. 1 Hut.

161

Sunday September 18th

Fine morning with a bright sun but cold in the shade & there was a hard frost during the night. Reveille was at 7:30 a.m. Breakfast at 8:30, Church parade at 11:15.

Fort Selkirk is situated opposite the junction of the Lewes & Pelly rivers, which form the Yukon river. Our camp is on the left bank looking towards the mouth, & is well situated, the ground being level with plenty of good timber within easy distance, & the water supply is all that could be desired. The scenery is not so mountainous as hitherto. Right opposite the camp the bank rises gradually at first, & then ends abruptly in a perpendicular wall of rock rising perhaps 150 feet sheer up & looking like a wall of solid masonry. It is evidently of volcanic origin, whilst away to the east rises the crater of an extinct volcano.

There is no settlement here as yet, but the Indians are very much in evidence. There is one store & mission church served by a missionary of the C[entral] M[issionary] S[ociety]. There is now, however, in camp a Provincial Govt. Survey party, who are, it is said, to lay out a town site, as it is intended to make this the capital of the district.

When we arrived last Sunday, we found building operations going on briskly. There are three large huts, each big enough to accommodate sixty or seventy men, besides Guardroom, Sgt.s' Mess, Officers' ditto, Orderly Room, QM & Supply Stores & Hospital, built in a parallelogram enclosing a fine parade ground. The buildings are now nearing completion & the work is being pushed on with all despatch. These huts are solidly constructed of logs, with double roofs, the intervening spaces being packed with moss. There are a large number of civilians working here, besides the soldiers & officers, & we hope to be all under cover by the end of the week.*

The Colonel has not yet returned from Dawson though there was another boat in late last night. There is no sign yet of our winter supplies & we have only about 25 days rations left. During the

---

* "The day following arrival of the Advanced Party at Fort Selkirk a site was selected for the Barracks and a lumber camp established about three miles above the Settlement, for the purpose of cutting and rafting down building logs .... A saw mill was found to be in operation

week all hands have been busy at all sorts of jobs. Some (myself amongst this number) getting in logs, some gathering moss, others employed as carpenters, sawyers, glaziers, clearing land, digging foundations, fencing, etc. I believe it is the intention to build a stockade or fence round the barracks at some future date. It is also intended to try & cultivate a portion of land adjoining, for the supply of fresh vegetables.

There are three N.W.M.P. stationed here, a sergeant & two constables.

Monday September 19th

First fall of snow today. Numerous parties proceeding down river in scows & boats. Dogs making an infernal row especially at night. Hard day's work & too tired to write more. Three steamers in.

Tuesday September 20th

Last night, about 'Last Post,' & after most of us were between

---

on the opposite side of the river which furnished lumber at reasonable rates. This mill closed down about the 1st October but the fortunate arrival of the Canadian Yukon Lumber Company, which erected a mill a short distance from the Barracks, enabled me to proceed with the completion of the buildings ... .The Barracks include three buildings 22 x 85 ft, 10 ft walls, occupied as Barrack rooms, Mess Room and cook house. Two buildings 22 x 85 ft — one used as a store house, and the other as Sergeants' Mess, Canteen and Recreation Room. Two buildings 28 x 70 ft, one used as a the Officers' Mess and the other as Hospital and Quartermaster's Stores. Three buildings 20 x 24 ft., of peeled logs, fronting on the river, used as Orderly Room, Guard Room and Cells and Commanding Officer's quarters. One building used as a Bakery 20 x 24 ft. In addition to the above, lean-to sheds were built in rear of the three Barrack Buildings for wash houses; a coal-oil shed and dog kennel in rear of the Bakery; winter latrines for Officers, Rank and File and Hospital, and also a Corral, 90 x 27 ft with 10 ft walls, built of poles and roofed, for the storage of 2,200 lbs of fresh beef purchased for the Force.

The failure of supplies and stores via St. Michael's to arrive at an early date added to the difficulties of construction and necessitated the manufacture by hand of all the window sashes required. A considerable amount of skilled civilian labour was found available at reasonable rates ... . The number of men on the civil pay roll may at first appear large, but on closer inspection it will be found that the majority were employed for a short period. In giving employment preference was shown to prospectors who had come across the Teslin Trail, many of whom were without money of food. When men of this class had earned sufficient to purchase enough food, etc., to make a start I discharged them in order to make room for others. Canadians or other British Subjects, were always secured when available. The general rate of wages paid was $5.00 per day without rations." — Evans to Adjutant-General, 1 November 1898, D Hist 73/78.

the blankets, we were suddenly aroused by the bugle sounding the "Assembly". Immediately all was bustle & confusion for a few minutes, as we had the order to turn out under arms. We got out very quickly, however, & fell in silently. Conjectures were many as to the cause of this sudden alarm for no one, not even the officers, knew. They could not even find out at first who sounded the call. After about ten minutes anxious waiting it transpired that the bugler of the guard heard the assembly sounded on one of the steamers & immediately repeated it. The whole affair appeared to have been a hoax.

Three steamers came in last night, on one of which was the Colonel with sixty days provisions & other stores; our other winter supplies being stuck somewhere below Dawson.* At work today cleaning up round the square & other odd jobs. After supper volunteers were called for to get a large scow off a bar. Extra pay guaranteed & I formed one of the party. We succeeded in getting her off in about 15 minutes.

Mail in today bringing two letters from my father dated July 22th & Aug. 5th, also several papers.

Wednesday September 21st

I was sent to join the moss party today. This is the softest job I have yet had although we have to go three miles to get to it morning & afternoon, making twelve miles in all.

The Colonel has returned to Dawson. We had steak & fresh potatoes for dinner. There was a little snow early in the morning & rain at night.

Thursday September 22nd

Same fatigue as yesterday — brought down a scow load of moss in afternoon. Raining all day. Sixty men are detailed for Dawson but only two from our half Company, viz Rogers & Platt.

---

* The supplies routed through Alaska via St. Michael's. The company which had contracted to bring them upriver — the Boston and Alaska Transportation Company — had collapsed financially. As a result, Capt. Pearse had "become personally responsible for the cordwood to keep the boats moving" and William Ogilvie (who had succeeded J.M. Walsh as Commissioner of the Yukon) had had to expend $8,000 to get the supplies moving again, including the charter of another steamer to fetch a barge abandoned some 600 miles downstream. — Ogilvie to Clifford Sifton, 22 September 1898, in Sifton Papers, PAC, MG 27, II, D 15, Vol. 295.

They will start early next week.*

Friday September 23rd

There was a heavy fog till about 11 a.m., after which it cleared & the rest of the day was very fine. Nothing worthy of remark occurred.

Saturday September 24th

Working all morning clearing land for garden. Drs. inspection & half holiday in afternoon. Day fine but cold.

Sunday September 25th

The week has passed so uneventfully that I have really next to nothing to write about. We have not been paid a cent yet & there is consequently a deal of quiet 'growsing' amongst the troops. However, I believe we are to be paid tomorrow, though whether up to date or not I cannot say. The weather during the week has been fairly good, though very cold at night with usually a sharp frost. There have also been several light falls of snow. We hope to move into the huts as soon as the Dawson detachment goes.

I have noticed that the farther we get North the poorer the type of Indians becomes. Those in the neighbourhood for instance are very low down in the scale of humanity. They are repulsively ugly & abominably dirty. They exist largely on fish & you can smell them a hundred yards off. They seem to be an idle, shiftless lot, & never seem to trouble about making the various little fancy articles for sale or barter which we saw amongst the Indians of the Stikine & Teslin Lake. The missionary holds a day school for these Indians, but does not appear to be very successful with his dusky pupils as only a very few words of English are spoken by even the most

---

* On 3 September 1898 the Adjutant-General's office in Ottawa had sent Evans a message ordering him to send half his force (including himself) to Dawson, but the message was signed by Clifford Sifton, the Minister of the Interior. Evans' loyalty lay with the Minister of Militia and Defence, so he ignored it. In any case, that signal only reached Fort Selkirk on 17 September and two days earlier Evans had responded favourably to a request from the Yukon Commissioner, Major J.M. Walsh, for the services of fifty NCO's and men by assigning the required force plus two officers —Captain H.E. Burstall and J.H.C. Ogilvie— and one of the Force's two Maxim machine guns to Dawson, where they would be accommodated in the NWMP barracks. - PAC, RG 9, B 1, Vol. 280, ff 76900.

intelligent.

The Pelly River, which joins the main stream right opposite the barracks, is a good sized stream & numerous parties are at present prospecting it & its tributaries. It is mainly in the expectations of the Pelly turning out well that the hopes of making Fort Selkirk a flourishing centre are based. If the Pelly does not turn up trumps, then goodbye to Fort Selkirk as the Capital of the Yukon district.

Monday September 26th

Our work today consisted first of hauling a scow ashore onto the flat, & then hauling logs from the bush half a mile above & floating them down to the barracks. We only worked till 3:45 p.m., on account of pay, which we received up to the end of June. I received $44.70 & Larose paid me for the revolver ($12.00). Day fine but cold.

Tuesday September 27th

Death visited the camp last night. On rising this morning we were surprised & shocked to hear Jerry Corcoran of the Garrison Artillery had been found dead in his tent. It seems that he came in last night late & somewhat 'under the weather' & tumbled into his blankets anyhow. When Bombardier Gavreau went to rouse him in the morning he was horrified to find him stiff & cold. He was in the best of health & spirits during the day. He leaves a sister in Quebec. The inquiry as to the cause of death was held this afternoon.

Today we were engaged in digging what is to be the garden in the morning. In the afternoon they wanted three men at a saw mill about half a mile up the river to do some work for them. I was one selected, we worked for three hours at $.30 per hour. We shall probably be required again tomorrow.

Wednesday September 28th

Today nearly all hands were cutting timber in the bush below the barracks & sawing it up into cordwood for our winter supply of fuel. We expected to work at the sawmill again, but another gang went down instead. The weather is much colder & there is no sign of the Dawson detail starting yet so we are still under canvas.

On guard tonight. Picquet sentry over mortuary tent.

Thursday September 29th
Corcoran buried today. The funeral procession started at 11:30 & was constituted as follows. Firing party, consisting of thirteen men from his own company; Bugle Band; Coffin, & upon it deceased's helmet, belt, & side arms; the whole of the Yukon Field Force. Lieut. Leduc conducted the service at the graveside. Between the volleys the bugles sounded the regimental call & after the last volley the "Last Post" was sounded.
Working in the bush in the afternoon.

Friday September 30th
In the bush all day. Thermometer 10° below.

Saturday October 1st
Today the Dawson party left by the steamer *Gold Star*, whilst we were working in the bush. In the afternoon we moved into No. 2 hut so we are now in comparative comfort. We are at present sleeping on the floor, but bunks are to be put in as soon as possible. The hut is warm & a great improvement on the tents now the weather has turned so cold. The whole of No. 3 Coy. are here, besides the remains of the Field Battery & the Cavalry. We were supposed to have a half-holiday today, but what with a fatigue & then moving in we did not have much time to ourselves.

Sunday October 2nd
Passed a most comfortable night being, if anything, too warm, as I am close to the stove, next to Cox & Arnotte. The stove is a large, sheet-iron, oil tank & big enough to take a three foot stick. The huts are 80 ft x 22 ft & built as elsewhere described.
Church parades as usual. There was a mail boat up but as I had no letter ready, had to let the opportunity slip. We received the welcome news of the arrival of our stores at Dawson. We also heard of the fall of Khartoum but could get no details. *

---

* On 2 September 1898 General Sir Herbert Kitchener's army — 26,000 men, about half of

167

Monday October 3rd

Thermometer 60 below. Working in the woods till noon. Short fatigue in the afternoon & then nothing more. This to make up for the loss of our half holiday on Saturday. Day bright & sunny but cold.

There are still numbers of people passing in to Dawson, but very few are now going out. Many of the former are traders taking in goods on scows, & some of them stop here & supply us with goods at somewhat cheaper rates than those we can get here. Prices are very high & the commoner the article the scarcer it seems to be, for instance, salt is almost as valuable as gold just now. In English money, Tobacco is 12/6 a pound, Milk 3/- a can, Candles 6d each, Sugar 2/6 per lb, Butter 5/- per lb, Eggs 4/2 per doz, Cigars 2/- each, Whiskey £ 1.12.6 per bottle, or 2/- a drink. Newspapers 2/- a copy, Ink 1/6 a small bottle, Golden Syrup 20/ per gallon, Pipes from 4/- etc.*

Tuesday October 4th

10° below during the night & very cold this morning. Still working in the woods. A boat called going up stream & Bombardier Kruger & Pte. Fleming, No. 2 Coy., went up to the Five Fingers to assist N.W.M.P. building operations.

Wednesday October 5th

Church parade for Catholics at 8 a.m. A Catholic priest having arrived from Dawson we had Requiem Mass & consecration of Corcoran's grave. Mass was said in our hut. The Father is staying over Sunday so we shall have Mass on that day. Work in the woods again this afternoon.

---

the British regulars and the remainder well-trained Egyptian troops— had broken the Khalifa Abdullah's horde of 40,000 fanatical dervishes at Omdurman, and taken the nearby Sudanese capital of Khartoum where General Charles Gordon had been slaughtered by the dervishes fourteen years earlier. As a cavalry subaltern, Winston Churchill participated in the charge of the 21st Lancers that cost the regiment a quarter of its strength but finally settled the battle.
*One pound sterling equalled approximately five Canadian dollars.

Thursday October 6th

Working in the woods all forenoon. In the afternoon I was one of a party hauling up and unloading a scow for N.W.M.P., for which we received $10.00, or $1.00 each. After that we drew an issue of clothing - viz. - 2 serges, 1 white canvas suit, 1 pr. moccasins, 1 suit underwear, 1 pr. felt boots, 1 muffler, 2 pair socks, 1 pr. black stockings, 2 pr. woolen mitts, 1 pr. Elk ditto - two pr. serge pants to come. Fine but cold in the woods all day.

Friday October 7th

Orderly man - not for parade till 9:00 a.m. & 2:30 p.m. Working around barracks all day.

Saturday October 8th

Hauling up a scow load of meat from below the old mission & unloading same. Doctor's inspection & half holiday although we had a short & dirty fatigue in the afternoon handling tripe (uncleaned). Waiting guard.*

Sunday October 9th

Flying sentry. During the afternoon three steamers came in from Dawson, one of which was laden with some or our winter supplies. This, of course, called for a fatigue for all hands & upwards of 150 tons of stores were brought ashore including the boxes containing our surplus kit. One of the St. Johns boxes was missing, & of course it proves to be the one in which my kit was, also Platt's, Dumas' & Hansen's. It will probable turn up on one of the other boats, one of which is high & dry forty miles down river.

The steamer in today, as soon as she has taken on wood, will return to the assistance of her consorts so we hope to have the remainder of our stores this week. A party was detailed to go on board the boat & proceed across the river to cut wood for her; they will probably work all night, receiving $0.60 an hour for the job. Received pay for work done week before last at saw mill.

---

* A waiting guard had no specific duties, but was available if another member of the guard fell sick, or if an extra man was needed.

Monday October 10th

Formed one of party sent to assist those cutting wood for boat, after which we were set to work carrying up stores from wharf to barracks using the H[udson] B[ay] straps, also a waggon & team & two small hand carts belonging to the B[ritish] A[merican] C[ompany].

I forgot to mention that two scows belonging to the N.W.M.P. came in yesterday, having on board several horses & seventy dogs. They are establishing post stations all along the route. They will leave some dogs here & the remainder will proceed towards Dawson tomorrow. The seventy dogs, with ours & the Indian dogs, succeeded in making the night hideous. I made the acquaintance of one of the police, Lovey by name. He is an Englishman & hails from Folkestone,* I am sending a letter to Jack Platt by him. The boys are busy tonight opening their kits. Brownlee has a violin on which he plays rather well. The weather is getting cold & we had a slight fall of snow this afternoon.

Tuesday October 11th

Finished getting stores up to barracks; they included fifty tons of flour & two 7-pounder mountain guns with several cases of shell.

The Colonel arrived on one of the boats last Sunday & today the two N[on] C[ommissioned] O[fficers] who were in Corcoran's tent when he died were 'put on the peg' & told off, with the result that Bombr. Marshall was severely reprimanded & Corp. Matthews put back for a District Court Martial which will be composed as follows: President - Maj. Young; Members - Cap. Gardiner, Capt. Thacker; Prosecutor - Cap. Bennett. Charged with neglect of duty in not reporting deceased drunk.

Wednesday October 12th to Friday October 14th

One day now passes so much like another that it is almost

---

* Probably Frank Lukey, born Folkestone, England in 1874, who had joined the NWMP in 1893 and was posted to the Yukon on 1 February 1898. He served in South Africa with the Imperial Yeomanry and subsequently re-joined the RNWMP in 1905, serving on and off until 1915. He died at Victoria, B.C., in 1946. — PAC, RG 18, Vol. 3398, file 2857.

impossible to record anything of interest every day.* As all the stores are now up we have returned to our old routine & I am again working in the Bush. On Wednesday I assisted in raising the flagpole, on which was hoisted the headquarters' flag of the Yukon Field Force, & Wesley hoisted the flag. On Thursday the D[istrict] C[ourt] M[artial] was concluded & the sentence promulgated today; to be reduced to the ranks & 25 days H[ard] L[abour], the latter part of which was remitted.

There were two mail boats in today, one up & one down, but I got no mail. I half expected one from Platt. The weather is now bitterly cold but there has been little or no snow.

Saturday October 15th

Working in woods all mornings in very cold weather. In the afternoon we had a drill after parade, what for no one seems to know as we were the only company for it & were merely inspected by Mr. Leduc & dismissed immediately. After this we had the afternoon to ourselves.

In the afternoon two steamers came in with more of our winter stores. We all had to turn out at 6 p.m. & worked till 11 p.m. unloading them bringing about 150 tons ashore. Amongst it I noticed our missing box. All this will have to be carried up to barracks next week so we are looking forward to two of three days hard work.

Sunday October 16th

Quiet day. Church parades as usual - guard this evening.

Monday October 17th

On guard. Men working bringing up stores.

---

* Life was livelier in Dawson. "At 6:05 Friday morning the police bugle sounded the emergency fire call in Dawson and in five minutes, half-dressed, unmounted police, soldiers of the artillery and infantry were running on the double to the Green Tree Saloon and Hotel, where black smoke and flames were bursting from the upper windows ... ." The ensuing conflagration burnt forty buildings to the ground and caused an estimated half-million dollars worth of damage. "There is no record of a fatality which is astounding. One member of the infantry occupied on the roof lost his footing and fell to the ground resulting in severe injuries and one convulsion after another. Another climbed a ladder to help tear down a burning building and the whole wall fell over on top of him. One was struck on the head by an axe carried by a

Tuesday October 18th

Helped carrying up stores. Finished about 3 p.m. & had rest of day to ourselves. The two 7-pounder guns have been mounted & placed on the river front so we present a very warlike appearance to anyone passing up or down.

Wednesday October 19th to Saturday October 22nd

Nothing worthy of mention has passed during the last four days. We were all struck off working pay & have to do 6 hours fatigue a day which really amounts to nothing, cleaning up & sawing wood. Special working parties, however, have been detailed for carpenters & builders, & for chopping cordwood in the bush. I am on the latter so still draw my working pay, for which am duly thankful. We work from daylight to dark, with an hour & half for dinner.

A twenty-four hour guard has been put on in place of the 12-hour guard & the flying sentry, & the companies have been reorganizing. Dawson detachment, No. 1 Coy.; Cavalry, Artillery, & London, No. 2 Coy.; Toronto, St. Johns, & Fredericton, No. 3 Coy.; Kelly & Kennedy in orders as Buglers.

Sunday October 23rd

Drs. inspection at 10 a.m. which the Catholics got out of. Weather has been much milder & it has been trying to snow all week but not much has fallen. Parties are still passing down towards Dawson in boats & scows but the water is getting very low & nearly all the scows which try to get through on this side get stuck.

Monday October 24th

Working as usual in the woods. It was snowing all day & very cold on the feet, the ammunition boots being very soon soaked with the snow water. A mail was in from Dawson & several letters were received. They all seem to have been on a 'toot' as a number of them, including Master Jack Platt, are doing C.B., * so of course I got no letter.

---

busy firefighter." — S.M. Flyke, "Holy Smoke!", in Andrew Baird, *Sixty Years on the Klondike* (privately printed, n.d.)

* "Enclosed I send you a copy of the *Canadian Military Gazette* dealing with the sins of two

The Yukon Field Force guarding the gold at Dawson. Nearly $400,000 (in 1899 prices) is in sight.

On guard at Fort Selkirk

Tuesday October 25th

Snow still falling & much colder & the country now looks more like what one would expect to find in the Klondike. The river is still open, though very low. No mail steamers have been down for some time. I am anxious to hear some news of my mother.

Last night there was a meeting for the purpose of considering the advisibility of forming a Social Club. I did not attend myself but was elected a member of the Committee in my absence. We are going to open on Hallowe'en with a smoker in the new dining room.

The following is an extract from the regimental order book dated 25.10.98:

"The undermentioned sleigh dogs having been purchased for the force are taken on the strength from the 24th inst:

Puff

Watch

Jip

Sancho

Carlo

By order etc."

Wednesday October 26th

Whole holiday today for the working party on account of some work done on Saturday afternoon. We received three months pay this afternoon, viz. July, August, & Sept. I received $83.30. Snowing all day.

Thursday October 27th

Snow continues to fall & weather not very cold, which renders work in the woods very unpleasant as the snow soaks through the ammunition boots like water through blotting paper & we have to

---

of three men gone wrong out of 200. One steals a keg of whiskey on a drunken spree and pays a far more severe penalty than had he been a civilian. Another, a country boy— Ryan— makes a break at the gambling tables & is finished [illegible] up. A third man, Platt, who served in the Bechuana Border Police and was with Jameson in his Raid has a soldier's holiday, gets drunk, has a fight and is punished, and although he has kept steady for seven months he now finds himself labelled a blackguard, and all this in a paper called 'The Gentlemen's Paper'." - Evans to H.J. Woodside, 17 July 1899, in Woodside Papers, PAC, MG 30, C 64, Vol. 31, file 1. The *CMG* customarily reflected the Active Militia's jealousy and resentment of the Permanent Force.

work for hours with wet feet. Darkness now compels us to knock off work at 5 p.m.

Friday October 28th

Guard today with Brownell & Dumas. Kelly, bugler, & Corp. Hansen in charge. Snowing all day. Lowest temp., 1 above.

Saturday October 29th

Coming off guard. Drs. inspection. No. 3 hut opened for dining & recreation room. Canteen opened - not much in it however.

Sunday October 30th

Church parades as usual. Fine day & no snow. River still open.

Monday October 31st

Snow in woods now pretty deep & it is still snowing. In the evening we had the opening concert of the newly formed Social Club, which, considering the short notice & the difficulties we had to overcome, was very successful. The hits of the evening were the song & recitation of Pte. Green, R.C.D, both of which were original.* The song was a parody of "Tommy Atkins" & the recitation was in imitation of Rudyard Kipling. It was so distinctly good that I am tempted to give it in its entirety. It is ....

[*Only a few isolated word are legible in the entries for the next three days. The diary resumes with the last three lines of the entry for Thursday, 3 November 1898.*]

... on the eve of the Colonel's departures for Dawson which will take place as soon as the river is fit for travel [by dog sled] probably in ten or fourteen days.

---

* Lester makes no mention of Trumpeter-Sergeant McKinnon, RCD, but Evans subsequently recorded that "The services rendered by this N.C. Officer during the past winter in assisting in the amusement and recreation of the Force were invaluable. With the assistance of instruments the property of N.C. Officers and men, the Bugles of the Force and two home-made drums, he organized a band which greatly added to the enjoyment of all ranks." The "home-made drums" were fashioned by Trumpeter Jacques who was "an excellent tinsmith, stove repairer, baker and cornet player" from cheese boxes and caribou skins. — PAC, RG 9, II, Vol. 284, ff 77933.

Friday November 4th to Sunday November 6th

Things progressing as usual. The weather has been very cold & the thermometer never above zero. Today I finished a long letter to my mother dealing with the journey from Ft. Evans to Ft. Selkirk.

Monday November 7th

Still working in the bush. River not yet frozen over but very near it, the channel nearest the barracks being solid.

Tuesday November 8th

Winter clothing issued, it is a splendid kit. Mail in from East. Letter from mother & seven weeks' papers.

Wednesday November 9th

When we turned out for work this morning we found the river completely frozen over. During the day the water rose, breaking up & piling the ice, cake upon cake, till the whole is like a river of rocks & frozen solid.

Thursday November 10th

River is rising in many places, flooding the banks. Bunks in hut almost completed, expect to get mine tomorrow.

Friday November 11th

On guard. Two parties with dog sleighs came down Pelly River. Report good gold prospects. Was talking with one of them who is an Englishman & knows Rotherhithe well. Pay for October $32.60.

Saturday November 12th

Coming off guard. Library opened in the evening. We have a small [illegible]. They include most of the standard authors such as Scott, Lever, Dickens, Kipling, Mayne Reid, George Elliot [sic], Besant, Marryat, Henty, Ballantyne, etc.

Sunday November 13th

Bakehouse fatigue, therefore not for church. Got my mother's letter ready for mailing.

Monday & Tuesday November 14th & 15th
Weather cold but not excessively so. Still working in bush.

Wednesday November 16th
Today was observed as a general holiday & thanksgiving day. We had a short religious service in the morning for all denominations. In the evening the second smoking concert of the Social Club was held. There was quite a large attendance of civilians.

The Colonel was to have gone to Dawson tomorrow but has postponed his departure till Sunday next. Major Bliss & the Sergt.-Major are to accompany him.

Thursday November 17th
Turned our white canvas suits & oilskins into stores. Weather bitterly cold. Therm. about 30° below. Some civilians who are going out of the country were camping in the bush near where we were chopping. They have no tent but are well supplied with blankets. Nevertheless, I don't envy them tonight with the temperature away down towards 50° below.

Friday November 18th
Fine but bitterly cold. Temp. 52° below all night. Never above 40° all day. On sick list in morning, in the bush after dinner. Got chin frozen.

Saturday November 19th
Temp. 50° below or thereabouts. Orderly man. * Many had ears, noses & chins frozen. Drs. inspection.

Sunday November 20th
Temp. at or about 40° [below] all day. Church parades changed, R.C. 9 a.m., C. of E. 10 a.m. Colonel Evans, Maj. Bliss, Capt. Bennett, S[ergeant]-M[ajor] Young & Pte. Docherty started for Dawson about 9 a.m. Read for first time *The Bondsman* by Hall Caine, was very much taken with it.

.

---

* Assisting the orderly sergeant during the latter's 24-hour assignment as routine administrator and minor "trouble - shooter" of the fort.

177

Monday November 21st

Temp. in night 45° below. Alteration in routine. Reveille 7:00 a.m., breakfast 8:00 a.m., parade at 9 a.m. Afternoon as before. Mail in this evening from Dawson. Longstreet had a letter from one of the boys; he says two of the men are being sent back here, no names mentioned & no reason for the move. Should not, however, be surprised if Jack Platt turns out to be one of them.

The guard at Fort Selkirk salutes the flag at the nightly "Retreat" ceremony

We cannot now work in the woods after 4 o'clock on account of darkness. It was below 40° all day but as there is no wind we are able to bear it. We light a roaring fire & knock off for a warm-up every fifteen or twenty minutes. If we did not do this we should soon get our feet frozen. I got my nose & chin slightly nipped today on the way home.

Tuesday November 22nd to Friday November 25th

The weather continued most severe till yesterday, when the thermometer rose & some snow fell, & today the temperature is about zero It is therefore comparatively mild.

Saturday November 26th
Weather still continues milder & snow is falling lightly. Drs. inspection at 1:15 p.m. As I thought, Jack was one of the two men sent back from Dawson, the other man was Quinn of No. 4 Depot. They were in the charge of Corp. Lawton who, however, will return to Dawson. They report a terrible journey over the ice, through which they went several times. They are all more or less

NCO's of No. 1 Company, in winter dress at Dawson.

179

badly frostbitten. They were fourteen days on the journey, ran out of grub, & altogether had anything but a lovely time. They give a bad account of the duties in Dawson & seem very glad to get back.*

Hockey match on a rink which has been made on the river. No. 2 vs. No. 3 . Comp[anies]; No.2 won, 1-0.

Sunday November 27th

Church parades as usual. Mailed letter to Cotton briefly describing march from Telegraph Creek.

Monday November 28th

Corp. Lawton returned to Dawson, accompanied by Ptes. Bateman & Burt. I hear from the Colour-Sergt. that I came near being selected, for which escape I am duly thankful. **

Tuesday November 29th

Put in for a pass this afternoon but it was not signed on account of some misunderstanding. Turning cold again.

Wednesday November 30th

Picquet. Much colder. Dog sleighs are now constantly passing

---

* In a diary which cannot now be located — R.C. Featherstonhaugh acknowledged the loan of it in the preface to his 1936 history of the Royal Canadian Regiment — Pte. Frank H. Freeland recorded one aspect of the Dawson detachment's duties. "Tonight I am on the duty of inside bank guard at the Canadian Bank of Commerce, from 7 p.m. until 7 tomorrow morning. At the appointed hour, I report myself at the side door, with rifle, bayonet, side-arms and ten rounds of service ammunition. Once inside, I am shown the contents of the vault — bars and bars of gold and small bags with nuggets of gold. I am told I am responsible for all I have seen. I am then handed a fully-loaded, 45-calibre revolver, with orders to use it if need be, and am shown an electric alarm-button, which rings a bell upstairs where the bank staff sleep, and in the Mounted Police guard-room. A cold lunch has been laid out for me and I am allowed to read and smoke, but on no consideration am I to sleep. If any of the staff goes out, I am given a signal, and a pass-word when he returns lets him in by the side door. As the night passes, I can hear the tramp, tramp of the sentry outside, but I am not in communication with him, as the heavy wooden shutters are closed and all doors are barred and locked. It is hard to stay awake in the small hours, but the loud snores of a heavy sleeper upstairs help some, and I managed to keep alert until I am relieved by the janitor about 7:10 a.m."
** "At Dawson the Guard and Escort duties were too heavy to permit more than a moderate amount of drill." — Evans to Chief Staff Officer, 23 November 1899, in PAC RG 9, II, B 1, Vol. 312. In her report to the VON headquarters, in Ottawa, Georgia Powell recorded that typhoid was a major problem. "— typhoid with pneumonia, with malaria, congestion of the liver, rheumatism, neuralgia, sore throat, discharge from the ears, and sore eyes ... . Nor was the sickness all, but the filth and the vermin ..." — Quoted in J.M. Gibbon, *The Victorian*

through. Drill order parade tomorrow, strong as possible. Am putting in a pass for the afternoon. Hockey match between Nos. 2 & 3 Coys; No. 3 won, 2-0.

Thursday December 1st

Drill order parade for all hands except the cooks and carpenters. After a few company movements on the square we marched out as far as the mission buildings, returning to barracks about 11 o'clock. On pass in the afternoon, walked up as far as the steamboat slough [?] with Graham. We found they had a man down with typhoid, from which, we learned, one of their men had died a few weeks ago. We walked upon the ice & returned by the trail through the back. It was a beautiful day, sun shining but very cold.

The detachment of the Field Force which 'mushed' from Selkirk to Dawson over the winter ice, 1898-1899

Order of Nurses for Canada 50th Anniversary, 1897-1947, (Ottawa, 1947), p. 32. Had Lester been posted to Dawson, it seems likely that his medical training would have ensured his employment in the hospital there.

Friday December 2nd

On guard with Lowe & Hare, Bugler Kelly, & Corp. Moore in charge. Thermometer 27 below & rising slowly. There was to have been a general kit inspection today but it was postponed.

Saturday December 3rd

Therm. rose to zero before we dismounted guard. Drs. inspection. Thermometer continues to rise & some snow fell. A few parties passed through during the day on their way out. Received news of the Colonel & party having reached Dawson; they seem to have had a very rough time of it. Corp. Lawton's party also heard of, doing well.

Sunday December 4th

Church parades as usual. Mailed letter home describing our daily life & giving some account of the barracks. Temperature still rising.

Monday December 5th

Thermometer rose several degrees above zero.

Tuesday December 6th

Very mild all day & this evening actually thawing. Drill order for tomorrow.

Wednesday December 7th

There has been such a rapid thaw that the drill order parade was cancelled on account of the state of the square, which was one enormous puddle, & leather boots were allowed to be worn. I am on a 'minor' charge for turning out with moccasins on, although there was no order against wearing them. I guess I shall come out all right. It is my first minor for over three years. Hope this thaw will not continue long enough to break up the river, or goodbye to all hopes of mail this side of Xmas. Our next concert will be on the 27th. Am just now reading the works of Augusta Wilson, *Bulah, Infidel, St. Elmo, & At the Mercy of Tiberias*. The latter two I have read, and liked *At the Mercy* fairly well. The other two I don't think much of.

Thursday December 8th

The weather still very mild & during the night some rain fell. There was an accident at the saw mill this morning. One of the men got his arm caught in the band & twisted round the shaft breaking it in two places. He is being attended by Dr. Foster.

My minor was dismissed this morning. A man came in the hut this evening who is going out of the country & returning; he is taking commissions. I have given him several orders, he expects to be back the first week in February.

Friday December 9th

A little colder & some snow fell. General kit inspection at 2 p.m. which passed off satisfactory. Did not go to work after.

Saturday December 10th

Drs. inspection as usual.

Sunday December 11th

Church parades as usual. I have now finished Augusta Wilson's novels & on the whole don't think much of them. *At the Mercy of Tiberias* is far away the best in my opinion. *Bulah* I have no use for at all. The heroine is a most disagreeable piece of goods who is thoroughly [illegible] herself for no earthly reason & persists in making everybody round her the same.

We expect the Colonel here very shortly as we have heard he is only a couple of days journey down. I suppose we shall be having a first draft for Dawson when he arrives. I sincerely hope it won't take me.

Monday December 12th

Weather getting colder. Therm. is somewhere in the vicinity of zero. The Colonel [and] Maj. Bliss arrived from Dawson this afternoon. We heard today that the mail which left here for the outside on the 22nd November has been lost through the ice, the dogs & even the mail carrier barely escaped with their lives. My long letter therefore is lost with the rest —several of the men have lost money which they were sending to their friends at home.

Col. Evans and his escort travelling between Fort Selkirk and Dawson. Evans second from right

Tuesday December 13th

Weather keeps moderate. Drill order at 10:00 a.m. March out about two miles returning to barracks about 11:30 a.m. Working as usual in the woods in afternoon. Committee meeting of the Social Club in the evening. Resolved next concert to be held on 27th inst. Good programme promised. Whist tournament being organized. Dumas & I have entered together.

Wednesday December 14th

Should have been orderly man today but Arnott took it over for me.

Thursday December 15th

Clock set back 45 minutes last night, by order of the Colonel, to make our time correspond with that of Dawson. It is now too dark to work at 3 o'clock & today we knocked off at 2:45 p.m. The sun rose today at 10:45 a.m. & set about 2:15 p.m. Extract from orders tonight, Hosp[ital]-Sergt. McIntosh to proceed to Five Fingers tomorrow with medicine to attend one of the N.W.M.P. who is sick.

Friday December 16th

Pay this evening for November at 8 p.m. $29.70.

Sunday December 18th

Usual Sunday routine. Getting colder. There was a hockey match yesterday. No. 3 Sect., No. 3 Coy. — No. 2 Sect., No 2. Coy. The latter won 1-0.

Monday December 19th

Picquet & prisoners' escort. Working in woods in afternoon. Am reading *Far from the Madding Crowd* by Thos. Hardy. At a special meeting of the Social Club Committee it was resolved to hold the next concert on the 23rd instead of the 27th inst., on account of the departure of the Dawson detachment on that date.

Wednesday December 21st

Guard with Meach & Hinsley, Kelly bugler, & Corp. Walters in command. Thermometer above zero all day but there was a nasty raw wind. Party with two dog teams passed through from Dawson who proved to be part of the English outfit I met at Teslin. They say they are thoroughly sick of the country & nothing will tempt them to come in again. Graham & I bought Longstreet's town lot for $25.00.

Thursday December 22nd

Therm. fell to 7° below last night — on pass in afternoon. Rehearsal for concert in evening.

Friday December 23rd

Wash-house fatigue. Therm. fell during the night to 8o below & remained low all day...

[Entries are either missing or illegible.]

Monday January 9th

Slight change in routine today. Usual fatigues in morning but in the afternoon worked from 1:00 till 2:30. Weather still mild.

Christmas dinner in the Dawson barracks. The Maxim gun was inside the messhall because the oil on its working parts would have frozen in the outside temperature.

Tuesday January 10th

Snow last night with a stiff breeze blowing from the N.W. which continued all day, rendering work in the woodyard very unpleasant, though the thermometer was never more than a few degrees below zero. They have taken to giving us a certain amount of wood to saw & we are dismissed when we have finished out task. We finished this morning at 11:30 & this afternoon at 1:50. I don't know how long this state of things will last but I am afraid they will increase our task if they find us getting through too fast. No sign of mail.

Wednesday January 11th

Waiting guard. N.W. wind still makes weather very unpleasant. Kit & Drs. inspection, fire drill. Skin coming off tops of my fingers where they were frozen which makes it very awkward for work.

First Christmas of the Yukon Field Force, 1899

Thursday January 12th

Guard today, Meach & Megan - Bug. Kennedy & Corp. Moore in charge. Unpleasant guard on account of wind. Thermometer 24° below. Read *White Rose* by Whyte Melville.

Friday January 13th

Last night did my sentry in one of the fur 'parkas' provided for the guard & very warm & comfortable I found it. It is a sort of fur shirt with a hood, unlined & very light & loose, keeping out the wind most effectually.

Saturday January 14th

Picquet with Platt & Megan. What I anticipated with regard to the wood fatigue came about all right. We had about four cords to saw & we worked hard at it, getting through about 11 o'clock. Instead of being dismissed, however, as we were led to suppose, we were ordered to carry up wood from the pile till the "Disperse" went. Curses deep, if not loud, were the natural result. This kind of treatment is doing incalculable harm to the temper of the troops

& is fast destroying what little good feeling is left between officers & men.

Hockey match in afternoon between Officers & Old No. 1 Section of No. 2 Coy. & all hands turned out for the purpose of expressing their feelings contra the officers who were beaten 1-0, hugely to the delight of 'Tommy'.

Sunday January 15th

C. of E. parade was at 10:30, Catholics at the usual hour. Orderly man. Book read - *Marooned* by Clark Russell.

Mr. Leduc & the S[ergt.]-M[ajor] expected in from Dawson tomorrow.

Monday January 16th

Usual fatigue. Mail from East in afternoon. Letter from Arthur, date Oct. 1st. It had been wet, was unsealed, & the stamp washed off. The letter itself was peculiar for its brevity considering it had travelled over 7,000 miles & had been nearly four months in transit. The little it did contain was not very cheering. I feel very much concerned about my mother's health & on that account I am glad we shall clear out of here this summer, otherwise I should be quite content to serve my full time up here. I received no papers but make no doubt they have been lost in transit.

Tuesday January 17th

Sergeant's Insp., fatigue. Docherty in orders, acting Corporal.

Wednesday January 18th

Kit & D[octo]rs inspection. Fire drill. Slight fall of snow. Another mail in today & I got two letters from Arthur & one from my father dated Nov. 11th & 22nd Nov. respectively. They were both written to inform me of my mother's slightly improved condition, but bad seems to be the best.

This mail, brought a lot of news from the various depots. The new general, Maj.-General Hutton,* has been making many

---

* Edward Thomas Henry Hutton was born in 1848 and commissioned into the 60th Rifles (King's Royal Rifle Corps) in 1867. He campaigned in South Africa (1879-1881) and Egypt

changes. At St. John's Sgt.-Maj. Phillips is to be retired in the spring as also is Quartermaster-Sergeant Kennedy. Drill Sgts. Roberts & Doxlader [?] are buying out. Other radical changes are also being made with regard to the other depots.

Major-Gen. Hutton has been speaking very highly of the "Field Force". The following is an extract from a speech delivered by him a short time ago. "General Hutton closed his speech with the following complimentary reference to the Yukon Field Force - "With reference to the Yukon Field Force, & this I want you to pay great attention to, the Y.F.F. is a representative force of Canada's troops, & they, in pushing their way to Selkirk, over very great physical difficulties achieved a great feat".

"They have in fact had an opportunity given them, which you & I would gladly have too, of showing that Canadian troops of today, Canadian soldiers of the present, are the equals of the Canadian soldiers of the past, that is the equal of the soldier of the 1885 campaign & are of that [illegible] campaign, in that [in] their march to the Teslin lake, & over very great physical difficulties to Selkirk & Dawson, they practically showed themselves the equals of the Red River Force as a pioneer force."

"In other words, Gentlemen, they showed themselves to possess a perseverance & persistence of purpose, an endurance & discipline under most trying circumstances, which we Britons consider to be a special prerogative of the British Army. Well now, I ask of you, bearing this in mind, as the Yukon Field Force is at the beginning of a very hard winter & will therefore have to undergo very great hardships, I say I will ask you to bear them in mind & with me give three good cheers for Colonel Evans, the Yukon Field Force & the Canadian Militia."

"Three cheers were given with great enthusiasm."

There seems to be a strong feeling in the Depots that some of us

(1882) before being appointed GOC, New South Wales (1892-96), AAG Ireland (1896-1898) and GOC Canada (1898-1900). His enthusiasm for an effective militia untainted by patronage failed to please the Laurier administration and he was recalled to Britain prematurely in response to a Canadian request. (See Desmond Morton, *Ministers and Generals* (Toronto, 1970). He commanded the Imperial Mounted Infantry in South Africa (1900), and then organised and commanded the military forces of the fledgling Commonwealth of Australia (1901-04). He commanded the 3rd Division of the BEF in 1914-15. Died 1923.

at least will be recalled in the summer if not too early [*sic*]. I hope this will prove to be true.

Thursday January 19th

Another fire this afternoon, strangely enough in precisely the same spot as that on the 1st inst. i.e. the roof of the orderly room. The boys turned out very smartly & it was only an affair of ten or fifteen minutes although it had started to blaze pretty fiercely, but it did not penetrate the inner roof.

Right half-Coy. issued with snowshoes. Several dog teams passed through today, both up & down, & one party went up the Pelly.

Friday January 20th

Snow falling. Lowe, Edwards & Walker went on ten days' furlough up the Pelly. They took a hand sleigh & ten days rations. Snowshoes issued & snowshoe parade for right half. Remainder of summer clothing issued.

Saturday January 21st

Cook-house fatigue. Hockey match in afternoon, No. 1 Sect., Old No. 2 Coy. vs. Winnipeg Contingent - final for the championship. Victory for "Gravel" [*sic*]. The latter rushed a goal in the first thirty seconds & then played a defending game till the finish, winning 1-0. The Colonel, who was a spectator only, interfered during the game & threatened to stop it if the infantry continued their defensive tactics. * This interference, even if the game was not being played fairly, was quite unwarrantable by a mere spectator & any objection should have come from the other side & have been decided by the referee. At all events the game played by the winning side was perfectly legitimate & was in fact the best tactics they could have adopted.

Sunday January 22nd

Orderly man. This morning about 5:45 a very distinct earth-

---

* Before taking command of the Field Force, Colonel Evans, it will be remembered, had been Officer Commanding 'B' Squadron, RCD - the "Winnipeg Contingent" of this entry.

quake shock was felt by many although it was not pronounced enough to awaken all. I for one did not feel anything of it, but those who were awake say that is shook things up considerably in the hut. This is the second that has occurred since we started on the trail, the first occurring whilst we lay at Telegraph Creek.

Monday January 23rd
Usual fatigues. Began to read "He Would Be a Gentleman" and "Terrible Temptation" by Chas. Reade.

Tuesday January 24th
Guard with Lefebvre and Lawsen; Kennedy, bugler, and Corp. Allen in charge. Thermometer down to 50° below. Two hours of sentry-go was as much as we wanted by the time we got through.

Wednesday January 25th
Just as we were being relieved from guard an alarm of fire was raised. This time it was the Officers' Mess blazing in the same old place. * The fire picquet got to work promptly & it was safe in about fifteen or twenty minutes.
Kit and Drs. inspection, also fire drill — rather superfluous after the events of the morning. Corp. Allen, Ptes. Graham, Meach & McIvor in orders to proceed to Dawson [on] Friday.

Thursday January 26th
Fire picquet. March out in afternoon on snowshoes, half way to farm and back. Pay for Dec. $30.80. Stuart in orders for [a] Stripe [promotion to L/Cpl].

Friday January 27th
Latrine fatigue. Snow falling. Dawson party did not start today. Snowshoe parade for R[ight] 1/2 C[ompany].

Saturday January 28th
Thermometer rose to zero and snow fell. Kit inspection for those who did not show Wednesday. Lowe, Edwards and Walker

---

* Apparently there had been one or more fires during the 23 December - 9 January period, for which the diary entries are missing.

returned from furlough. The Colonel and Capt. Thacker & party started for Dawson. Sent letter and papers to Arnott at Dawson.

Sunday January 29th
Usual services. Temp. about zero. Snowing. Started keeping Bell's diary.

Monday January 30th
General fatigue at 9 a.m. Mail in & I received a letter from my father dated Oct. 8th, also *Tid Bits* and *Manchester Weekly Times* & *The Regiment*.

Tuesday January 31st
General fatigue at 9 a.m. I was, however, on bakehouse fatigue. Fire in Q.M. Stores, out in a few minutes. As usual, it started round stove pipe. Wrote to my mother.

Wednesday February 1st
Orderly man - fireman on duty. General fatigue at 9 a.m. Kit and Dr's. inspection.

Thursday February 2nd
Fire again last night, just after 'Last Post'. This time it was in the Sergeants' Mess. The cooks got it out almost before we arrived on the scene. I was picquet sentry over it till the Orderly Officer came round, for which I was let off parade this morning. Mail in from [the] East but nothing for me.

Friday February 3rd
Picquet. Snowshoe tramp for the Left Half [Company] to steamboat slough & back.

Saturday February 4th
Guard with Lowe & Lefebvre. Kelly bugler and Langille in charge. Fine day & thermometer never below zero. You can now feel some warmth in the sun & the days are getting much longer. It is light at 8 a.m. and it is not dark until nearly 5 p.m.

Sunday February 5th

Church parade at the usual hours. Weather still mild (zero).

Monday February 6th

Latrine fatigue. Weather colder, 28 degrees below in night. Bright and sunny.

Tuesday February 7th

Mail in. Letter from Ethel dated Nov. 27th informing me of M's mother's death & also of the death of Harry Williams. She also tells me she is sending her photo but I did not receive it by this mail. I also received a letter from Arthur dated Dec. 2nd.

Wednesday February 8th

Fireman on duty. Drs. inspection this morning at hospital. No fatigue - kit inspection & fire drill in afternoon.

A civilian was run in by the police for cruelty to a horse & lodged in our guardroom. Inspector Scarth will weigh him off tomorrow. * The inspector arrived yesterday.

Thursday February 9th

Prisoner awarded $10.00 fine & costs. Washhouse fatigue. Snowshoe tramp for Right Half[-Company]. Wrote Cotton & Ethel. Don't know when the mail will go out so shall not mail them yet. 30° below.

Friday February 10th

Snowshoe parade for Left Half[-Company] at 1.30 p.m. Weather milder but a cold wind blowing.

Saturday February 11th

Orderly man. Usual half holiday.

---

* NWMP officers were also magistrates. William Hamilton Scarth was born in Toronto in 1870, graduated from the Royal Military College, Kingston in 1889 and was appointed Inspector in the NWMP on 15 October 1889, the youngest officer ever commissioned into that Force. He served in the NWMP for twelve years, was granted a six month leave of absence in 1901 to go to the South African War, and subsequently resigned to take a captaincy in the South African Constabulary. He served in South-West Africa and the European theatre during the First World War, then went into business in South Africa. In 1928 he returned to Toronto, where he died in 1935. — PAC, RG18, Vol. 3441, file 096

Sunday February 12th
Church as usual. Church fatigue.

Monday & Tuesday February 13th & 14th
Shrove Tuesday guard [with] Lefebvre, Lowe. Kelly, bugler [and] Sgt. Naufts in charge. Temp. zero.

Wednesday February 15th
Ash Wednesday. Kit & Drs. inspections - general holiday.

Thursday February 16th
Snowshoe tramp for Right Half[-Company]. Have been reading *The Miserable Many*, by Robert Barr. I remember reading part of it when it appeared in *Tid Bits* under another title. Think it very good.

Friday February 17th
Took Hudson's place as Hospital Orderly, Hudson being sick. Corp. Hansen has been in for some time & I was shocked to see the change in him. I don't think he will ever see St. John's again.

Saturday February 18th
Hansen was much worse this morning & died in his sleep at 3.15 this afternoon. I, with the assistance of Moreau, washed & laid him out.
The Colonel, with Cap. Thacker, returned from Dawson this afternoon.

Sunday February 19th
No church parade for me. Weather beastly cold & a high wind blowing - almost impossible to avoid getting exposed parts of body frozen.

Monday February 20th
Mail went out East taking my letters to Ethel & Cotton.

Tuesday February 21st
Corp. Hansen's funeral took place at 10.30 a.m. in bitterly cold

weather, the thermometer registering 64° below (in town). The firing party was taken from the men of his own section.

Hospital kitchen started, with Higgins as cook. Pay for January, $21.55. Mail in - three letters - two from Arthur - Oct. 21 & Nov. 4th, & one from my father, Oct. 15th. Our thermometer registered 57° below. Gunner Davies came into hospital with scurvy. *

Wednesday February 22nd

Walters who has been in hospital for some time is much worse & delirious. I sat up with him last night & McGill, who is convalescent after scurvy, is to sit up tonight. Not quite so cold.

Thursday February 23rd

Snowshoe parade for Right Half[-Company]. Walters about the same.

Friday February 24th

Snowshoe parade for Left Half. I am now fit.

Saturday February 25th

Instrumental concert in dining room in evening. Signed pay sheet for February.

Sunday February 26th

Baldwin came in hospital with lumbago.

Monday February 27th

No improvement in Walters. He is very low & quite unconscious. Has to be fed & relieved artificially.

---

* Evans reported to Ottawa that the health of the Selkirk detachment was "not satisfactory" due to the lack of fresh or tinned vegetables. "To prevent scurvy in this climate a certain proportion of tinned vegetables — tomatoes being the best —is necessary when fresh vegetables are not available." The health of the Dawson detachment, where more supplies were available, was good, but there were eight cases of typhoid among the men there, four of them being hospital ward orderlies. — Evans to Chief Staff Officer, 23 November 1899, in PAC, RG 9, II, B 1, Vol. 312. Why the lime juice brought in by the Force had not prevented scurvy developing is not clear, but it may be that the exchange of a keg of lime juice for an "equal volume of syrup", authorized by Evans at Glenora (Evans to OC Canadian Militia, 11 October 1898, in PAC, RG 9, II, B 1, Vol. 276, f. 75517) was a major error.

Tuesday February 28th

Walters died at 1.45 a.m. Auction of kits in the afternoon. Order came out for all wood [to] be drawn for barracks by dog sleigh.

Wednesday March 1st

Walters' funeral at 1 p.m. There was a fire in the morning, in the Officers' Mess. This time...[illegible]... but it did not amount to anything.

Thursday March 2nd

Hudson discharged from hospital & I was returned to duty. Mail in from East, nothing for me. Snowshoe tramp & social this evening to which I did not go.

Friday March 3rd

As I have not yet been officially returned to duty did not go on parade this morning.

Saturday March 4th

Public auction of Pte. Walters' kit. Cook house fatigue with Larose. Mail goes East tomorrow and am mailing letters to Mother & Ethel. Paddy Ryan, N.W.M.P. * a friend of [illegible] carries it out.

Sunday March 5th

Orderly man. Church as usual. Weather fine & bright but very cold. We now have a good twelve hours continuous daylight.

Monday March 6th

Change in working. Reveille, 6.30. Breakfast, 8.0. Drill, 9.30 to 10.30. Fatigue, 11 to 12.30. Dinner at 1 p.m. Fatigue, 2 to 5. Platt & Quinn on special fatigue in supply stores morning & afternoon. Mail in [with] letter from Arthur giving up all hopes of my dear mother. She is quite unconscious so I am now prepared for the worst.

---

* Patrick Joseph Ryan, born in Newfoundland, circa 1866, served in the Chilean cavalry during one of that country's many revolutions before joining the NWMP in 1888. Promoted corporal in 1900, he purchased his release in 1907, rejoining (the RCMP) as a special constable in 1932 and subsequently serving as saddler to the Musical Ride until 1952. Died Ottawa, 1958. — PAC, RG 18, Vol. 3380, file 2223.

Tuesday March 7th

Cook house fatigue with Matthews. C.O.'s parade at 9.30. Walking out dress with haversacks. March out as far as the lightening slough. Each man carried a ration of bread & meat. Cockburn preceded us with materials for brewing tea. The day was brilliantly fine, the sun shining brightly & not a cloud in the sky. Thermometer showed 30° below. We reached the slough about 11.50 & had lunch, getting back to barracks about 3 p.m. Distance traversed, about sixteen miles.

Wednesday March 8th

Fireman on duty. General kit & Drs. inspection.

Thursday March 9th

Picquet with Lefebvre & Low, Sgt. Bingham in charge.

Friday March 10th

Guard with Lowe, Lefebvre. Kelly, bugler, & Corp. Langille in charge. The whole guard [was] from St. John's, including prisoner (Billy Fowler).

A series of snowshoes races are being brought off just now. A Depot races teams of not less than four men, first three to count. Course: across river to top of the Pelly bluff & back. First heat today

Winnipeg	Team	time	
1st Corp.	Voss.	"	40.54 $^1/_3$
2nd Pte.	Green	"	44.20
3rd Pte.	Steer.	"	50.20
Average:		"	44.54 $^1/_3$

Saturday March 11th

Therm 9° above when we dismounted guard. Snowshoe competition - Second Heat - Third Heat

Field Artillery	time	
1st Hosp. Sgt. McIntosh	"	38.30
2nd Bug[ler]-Sgt. McKinnon	"	40.45
3rd Sgt. McCuly	"	45.30
Average:	"	42.08

197

Garrison Artillery

1st Gnr. Kingwell	time	39.10
2nd " Hurley	time	41.20
3rd " Mooney	time	41.40
Average:		40.45 1/3

Mail goes East tomorrow. Mailing letter to Arthur.

Sunday March 12th

Sgts. Mess fatigue which I swapped with "Sammy".

Monday March 13th

Orderly man. 4th & 5th Heats of snowshoe competition:

St. Johns	time	
1 Moreau	"	37.45
2 Cox	"	39.35
3 Bell	"	48.15
Average:	"	41.51 2/3

London not in it - no time taken.

Tuesday March 14th

March out up the Pelly in snowshoes. Beautiful day & sun quite hot. Mail in from East - Letter from Cotton. 6th Heat of snowshoe race:

Fredericton		
1 Quinn	time	34.35
2 _____	"	35.40
3 _____	"	35.50

This finishes the first round & the 1st & 2nd in each depot get a prize. First three in each race run in final for which there are five prizes. There is also a prize for the depot which gets most places in the final. Decided tomorrow.

Wednesday March 15th

Another grand day. Usual fatigue. Final of snowshoe competition decided this afternoon.

1st Corp. Voss	time	34.10
2 Gnr. Kingwell		

3 Pte. Moreau)
4 " Cox)   St. John's
5 " Bell)

The St. John's team therefore got the depot prize of one hundred cigars, having all three men placed. Short snowshoe tramp in the evening followed by the usual social & distribution of prizes. St. John's did well, receiving five prizes & Depot Championship.

Thursday March 16th

Fine day & quite warm. Usual routine; Greatcoat condemned. Colonel went to Dawson.

Friday March 17th

St. Patrick's Day. Twelve months today since re-enlistment. The weather is now really like spring. The sun warm & the snow fast disappearing from the mountain sides. March in walking-out dress without furs. Marched nearly to farm. Sgts'. Mess fatigue. Many parties are now passing through towards Dawson.

Saturday March 18th

Wet & scrubbed the huts today. Fatigue 10.00. Mail from East — Nothing for me.

Sunday March 19th

Today has been the finest day we have had this year. Bright, hot, day & cloudless sky, & the air mild, so much so that the water is dropping through the roofs of the huts. If this weather continues it will soon make short work of the river which they say is already open in parts.

Rumors are still flying round of our going out this summer but nothing definite has yet come to light. Mail went East this morning but I sent nothing by it. Church fatigue.

Monday March 20th

Was on a minor offence today for being late for Church fatigue yesterday. Harvey, Hennessy & P. Kelly were also up - admonished. Walked up to the slough yesterday evening with Cox, Platt & Jack Kelly.

Tuesday March 21st

Much colder - Picquet - Mail in, nothing for the force.

Wednesday March 22nd

Kit & Drs. inspection. Instrumental concert & "Stag" again in the evening. The thermometer is again down below zero but the weather fine.

Thursday March 23rd

Guard [with] Lefebvre & P. Kelly; Fournier, bugler, & Sgt. Beaumont in charge. Milder & thermometer rose to 18° above. Towards evening the wind dropped & the thermometer fell to 20° below. Several parties passed out & two dog sleighs, each with a man & a women, going into Dawson.

Friday March 24th

Company went for snowshoe tramp towards farm, carrying a ration of bread & meat. Returned about 1.30. Dinner at 2. As I was coming off guard I was not for it.

Saturday March 25th

Sgt's. Mess fatigue. Scrubbed out hut. Paraded for inspection of summer clothes. Weather colder, 30o below at reveille.

Sunday March 26th

Usual Sunday services.

Monday March 27th

Last Friday a corporal of N.W.M.P. stationed at Five Fingers attempted to commit suicide by cutting his throat.* Dr. Foster was instructed to go up & see him and this evening he was brought back & lodged in our hospital. I have been detailed to watch [him] at night.

---

* Andrew Lowry Holmes, born at Dacre, Ontario in 1865, enlisted in the NWMP in November 1889. No charge was laid against him in respect of this attempted suicide, it being held that he was temporarily of unsound mind — he was suffering from scurvy — at the time. Holmes was subsequently promoted to sergeant and was still serving in the Yukon, at Fortymile, when he died of heart disease on 12 January 1905. — PAC, RG 18, Vol. 3384, file 2373.

Tuesday March 28th

Lying off all day on account of sitting up all night. The patient has not injured himself much but he is slightly ratty. Pretty quiet during the night but tried to get out of bed twice this morning. He will have constant watching. Company marched out on snowshoes.

Wednesday March 29th

[Dr.] Foster & I sat up all night with Corp. Holmes. Sutures inserted into wound. Snowshoe tramp & social in evening. Cox, I, Roussell, & Megan sang "Glorious Apollo" as a quartette. Major Bliss arrived just after supper. He brought in some official mail the purport of which has not yet transpired.

Thursday March 30th

Still employed in hospital at night. Patient very quiet & seems quite rational.

Friday March 31st [Good Friday]

General holiday — no parades, not even church parade. Roll call in huts at 9.30 a.m. Fine day & quite warm S.E. wind. Snow fast disappearing.

Saturday April 1st

Day broke at 4 a.m. this morning showing that the days are now getting long. Watching all night in hospital. Holmes seems all right now & doesn't really require such constant supervision. However, I don't grumble as it gives me the whole day to myself.

A mail came in this evening but I got nothing. Roussell got a letter from Hebert at St. John's, he tells us that Yvonne [sic] whom I used to know in Montreal is dead, she died of consumption. She did not look a consumptive subject. I am sorry as she was a very nice girl.

Today has been the warmest this year, the thermometer going as high as 60° in the sun, & of course the snow was thawing rapidly all day. Leather boots had to be worn on the morning fatigues.

Sunday April 2nd

Easter Day. No Catholic service in consequence of no officer being present. Pelly [River] reported open in places.

Monday April 3rd

No drill parade. Fatigues instead & half holiday. Two mails in. Two letters from Arthur dated 12th & 19th Feb. respectively. They brought me the sad news I have been expecting. My dear mother died at 9 p.m. Feb. 11th. I was very grieved but it will not come as a shock as the letters from home prepared me for it. What I am now fearful of is that it will break up my father. However, Arthur says that although, of course, he feels it very much he is bearing up well, & I sincerely hope he will continue to do so. The mail from Dawson also came in and as it starts out tomorrow I wrote at once to my father.

Tuesday April 4th

Another glorious day. The square is now getting very sloppy. If it is any worse tomorrow I don't think we shall be able to have the usual square drill which has now been going on since March 6th. Company marched out strong as possible at 9 a.m., in sweaters, returning about noon.

Wednesday April 5th

Still thawing during the daytime & the square is one vast puddle. The Indians began their exodus today, a sure sign of spring. Many parties going up the Pelly where they will stay for hunting & fishing when the river breaks up. Usual Company Kit & Drs inspection in the afternoon.

When Maj. Bliss came in he brought with him a camera supplied by the department [of Militia and Defence] for the use of the Force. They are taking a series of pictures of the barracks & of the men in winter dress. For this purpose there is a parade at 9.30 tomorrow.

Thursday April 6th

The whole company paraded at 9 a.m. in drill order (winter dress) & were photographed, first on the square in line & in quarter column with guns & Maxims.* We then marched onto the river & were taken on the march & in action in skirmishing order with Maxims on the left & guns on the right flank, the right half-company representing the fighting lines & the left the reserves.

I was sitting up with Holmes all night. There was a magnificent display of the Northern Lights commencing about 10.30 & lasting till nearly midnight — from over the mountain to the North rose a pillar of light, gradually widening out fan-like, rolling round upon itself in endless coils towards the zenith & looking like a huge cone of fire, then suddenly breaking up & spreading over the whole of the Northern sky, thinning out & disappearing into a sort of luminous mist. Then from the whole of the Northern horizon arose beams and rays of light shooting & darting upwards in a magnificent arc, corruscating with prismatic colours, one line flaming up & illuminating the whole Northern hemisphere & again dying away, till only here & there could a stray beam of light be seen; then again flaming up in shafts & arrows of white, glistening light, rolling along the horizon like waves breaking upon a shelving beach, & so on again & again in ever-changing variety, a marvelous sight & one hardly to be described in mere words. By midnight not a trace of all this was to be seen.

Summer dress taken into wear for barracks, service caps & mackinaw for walking out. Ammunition boots at all times & fur caps after Retreat.

Friday April 7th

General fatigue for company in the morning. Weather still continues warm during the day but there is a hard frost at night, the thermometer usually going down to the vicinity of zero but seldom below. Corp. Holmes is now convalescent, so I go back to duty tomorrow.

Saturday April 8th

Orderly man. Colonel Evans with Corp. Docherty, Cockburn & Peel returned from Dawson about 12.30 p.m. Working all morning in Q.M. store tent. Some rain fell during evening.

---

* Apparently the Maxim gun which had been sent to Dawson in the fall had now been brought back to Fort Selkirk.

Part of the Field Force on parade at Fort Selkirk. The buildings behind them are those which they built themselves

Sunday April 9th

Another fine day. Church parades as usual.

Monday April 10th

Parade at 9.30 a.m. Arms drill by numbers. Summer dress. Pay in afternoon for Feb. & March.

Tuesday April 11th

Orderly man. Guard & picquet mounted in red [i.e. scarlet dress tunics]. Work this morning with pick & shovel, drill in afternoon. Mail went out. Sent letter to my father. On account of the state of the river it is very doubtful if this mail ever goes out.

Wednesday April 12th

Hospital fatigue. C.O.'s parade in drill order; march out over lake, past farm, two miles, returning about 12.30. Docherty started for Dawson. Afternoon, general kit & Drs. inspection & fire drill.

Thursday April 13th
At work with picks digging new refuse pit.

Friday April 14th
15 men detailed to work in woodyard from 9 to 10.30, of which I formed one. From 11 to 12.30 working in refuse pit & also from 2 to 3.

Saturday April 15th
Picquet with Lowe & Lefebvre. Mail in from East but only a few for the Force. General scrub out [illegible]. Orders tonight. New routines commence Monday. Reveille, 6; Breakfast, 8; Physical drill, 9 to 9.30. Arms drill, 9.40 to 10.30. Company drill, 11-12; Dinner; 12.30. Fatigue 1.30 - 3.30.

Sunday April 16th
Waiting Guard - cold day & slight fall of snow. Sight hailstorm in afternoon.

Monday April 17th
Reveille at 6 [illegible]...had all disappeared by noon. Guard with Dumas & Matthews, Walsh, bugler, & Sgt. Beaumont.

Tuesday April 18th
Coming off guard. Woodyard in afternoon. Guard mounted in marching order.

Wednesday April 19th
General fatigue from 10 to 12:15 cleaning snow & ice from, & draining, the barracks square. Kit inspection, etc., in afternoon. Snowshoes turned into stores.

Thursday April 20th
General fatigue in morning. Capt. Thacker sent for me off fatigue & asked me to go as servant to the Commanding Officer. I refused at first but was finally persuaded. There was a concert in the evening.

Friday April 21st

Usual parades. Edson left cookhouse and Chapman took it over.

Saturday April 22nd

Weather still fine & warm. The river is getting very swifter & breaking up in places but no signs yet of a break up.

Sunday April 23rd

Sharp shower of rain in the afternoon. Mail from East, nothing for me.

Members of the Dawson detachment drilling in the NWMP compound at Dawson (wearing summer workdress)

Wednesday April 26th

C.O.'s parade. Battalion drill. [illegible] helmets issued.

Thursday April 27th

Physical drill with arms. Guard picquet mounted in helmets.

Friday April 28th

Snow falling heavily at Reveille ....

[The remainder of this entry is indecipherable and there are no further entries.]

POSTSCRIPT
CHARACTER AND CIRCUMSTANCE

W hy the Lester diary stops as abruptly as it began, we do not know. It may be that boredom inclined the author to abandon it, just as variety had inspired him to start writing, eleven months earlier. Certainly, no salient change occurred in his circumstances which would have compelled him to change his habits at the end of April 1899. During the spring and summer of that year, Colonel Evans reported:

> The Force was trained, as far as possible, in the work pertaining to the respective branches of the Service of which it is composed. Classes in Topography, Flag Signalling and Stretcher Bearing were formed. Tactical exercises were carried out weekly in the country surrounding Fort Selkirk and a keen interest was displayed by all ranks ... . A rifle Range was constructed where the C[anadian] M[ilitary] R[ifle] League matches were fired and a limited amount of musketry work was done. The Range having been cut through the woods, the mosquitoes and sand flies made accurate shooting or good practice very difficult.

> ... a series of Cricket, Football and Rounders matches were arranged by the Regimental Amusement Committee ... . The Regimental and Company gardens were very fruitful, providing fresh vegetables for all messes.[1]

The Klondike stampede was over and mining was becoming big business. Steam dredges were already taking the place of rocker-boxes and muscle power, and the population of the Territory was dropping almost as rapidly as it had risen. As early as 12 November 1898, William Ogilvie, the one-time Dominion surveyor who had succeeded Walsh as Yukon Commissioner at the end of July and, in the ensuing four months, brought the administration of the district up to par, had informed Ottawa that:

We do not deem it necessary here to have any more of the militia in attendance, and I would respectfully submit that neither the Council nor myself consider the presence of the militia in the country necessary at all ... . The people here are peacefully inclined when properly dealt with. That is evident to every person. If they have been exasperated in the past there has been some reason for it, and today it is universally conceded by all right-thinking people that there is perhaps no more peaceable and orderly town in Canada than the town of Dawson. As for a rebellion, the time for that is past and gone. Last spring there was undoubtedly a crowd of discontented people here who hung about Dawson, waiting for something to turn up. They did not get what they expected, nor did they get what in some instances they might have got with perfect propriety. This exasperated them to such a degree that a little more would have raised a rebellion.[2]

General E.T.H. Hutton — who had succeeded Herbert as GOC Canadian Militia — was pleading for the return of the Field Force in order that his militia might be properly trained,[3] and in July 1899 the government finally accepted that the Yukon establishment might safely be halved. Apparently national prestige was no longer as important as it was when the decision to send troops in had been made, eighteen months earlier. American permission was requested — and granted — for up to one hundred soldiers not bearing arms to leave the Yukon via the White Pass and Skagway.[4] Their personal weapons were shipped as baggage in bond.

Five men purchased their release locally, and four officers — Major Young, Captains Burstall and Ogilvie, and Lieutenant Leduc — and 92 men left Selkirk on 8 September. They arrived in Vancouver on the 18th. It had taken the Force four months to reach

Selkirk from Vancouver, but half of them made the return journey in ten days, *via* Lake Bennett, the White Pass and Skagway. Two, perhaps overcome by the fleshpots of civilisation, deserted in Vancouver.[5]

Hardly had they left when the headquarters of the Force was shifted to Dawson on 5 October, leaving only a 'care and maintenance' detachment of nine men under Sergeant Lawson at Selkirk. Edward Lester must have been pleased (judging by his earlier diary entries) to find himself among the nine. It would seem that his appointment as Evans' servant did not extend beyond September, for Evans, of course, remained at Dawson for the few weeks that he remained in the north.

In South Africa the Boer republics, their ultimatum demanding the dispersal of British forces massing along their borders having been rejected, launched a pre-emptive attack on the British forces on 11 October 1899. By the 13th Boer commandos were laying siege to Kimberley and Mafeking; and on that same day the Canadian government, under tremendous pressure from the pro-Imperial part of the electorate, announced that a volunteer infantry contingent, 1,000 strong, would be sent to support the British. The men were recruited from the ranks of the Volunteer Militia across the Dominion, but all of the senior officers and a cadre of junior officers and other ranks were taken from the Permanent Force. Two of the officers who had left Selkirk in September, Burstall and Leduc, were among the regulars appointed to strengthen this First Contingent.

Under such circumstances, Evans was too senior to be left in command of a northern backwater, far from the mainstream of events. He was replaced in early November (and promptly appointed to command one of the two mounted rifle battalions being formed as a Second Contingent for South Africa), by Major T.D.R. Hemming, RRCI. Evans, too, went out over the White Pass, travelling by dog team to Skagway on 28 November 1899.[6]

For another seven months the Yukon Garrison, as the Force was now styled, continued to provide a military presence in the north, its duties now entirely limited to guards, picquets and fatigues, and dousing Dawson fires, (there was a particularly bad one on 10 January 1900) with the occasional ceremonial parade.

At Selkirk the monotony was doubtless eased by the absence of officers and the relative freedom from disciplinary harassment (the 'keep the men busy and they won't have time to get into trouble' syndrome) but Lester must have been happy to get away from the army entirely for a few weeks in February and March. A Mounted Policeman at Big Salmon River, 160 kilometres upstream from Fort Selkirk, had frozen two toes. Lester volunteered to go and nurse him and left, in the company of Inspector Scarth, at midnight on 10 February. Constable Walter Tyrrell's toes eventually had to be amputated but Assistant-Surgeon L.A. Pare of the NWMP noted that "Dr. Madore is perfectly competent to operate with the help of Private Lincoln of the Yukon Field Force, who was acting Hospital Sergeant at Fort Selkirk for the last few months and who went through the whole curriculum at Guy's Hospital, London... ."[7]

Fort Selkirk was finally abandoned in May 1900, when Lawson's little detachment moved down to Dawson. By then Lester had been promoted to corporal, presumably in recognition of his medical and nursing skills. And, at that time, apparently he forgot or misplaced his diary, leaving it jammed between a couple of rough-hewn logs in a barrack wall.

In Ottawa, the Minister of Militia had already advised the Cabinet that there was no longer any good reason to keep troops in the Yukon and the final withdrawal of the Yukon Garrison was announced. On 25 June 1900 all but one member of the Garrison embarked for Whitehorse on the S.S. *Columbian*, leaving their personal weapons and winter clothing with the Dawson NWMP detachment. From Whitehorse they marched over the Pass to Skagway, sailing from there on 3 July and reaching Vancouver two days later.[8] The uniforms, rifles and two Maxim guns were subsequently used to equip a Volunteer Militia unit, the Dawson Rifle Company, which was formed in July 1901. The two 7-pounder field guns, one of steel and one of brass and both absolutely useless for anything other than ceremonial purposes, remained with the 'Mounties' and can still be seen to this day, adorning the RCMP office at Dawson.

The one member of the Garrison who did not leave Dawson was Corporal Edward Lester, alias Lincoln. He stayed on, boarded and fed by the police, "as he was required as an important witness in the case of the Queen vs O'Brien, held for murder."[9] In one of the Yukon's most famous trials, George O'Brien was subsequently convicted of the murder of Lynn Wallace Relfe on Christmas Day 1899. O'Brien, together with an unidentified accomplice who was never caught, killed Relfe and two other men on the trail between Minto and Hootchiku, two tiny settlements some thirty-five to forty kilometres downstream from Selkirk, their motive being simple robbery.

The partly decomposed bodies were not found until the spring thaw exposed them. An intense investigation then began and eventually produced enough circumstantial evidence to convict O'Brien. What Lester's contribution might have been we do not know, for although the police at one time considered him "an important witness" he was never called upon to testify.[10] Some of the evidence against O'Brien was medical and scientific and it may well be that the 'Hospital Sergeant' from Fort Selkirk — the nearest man with medical training, whose skills were now well known to the police on the upper Yukon — was incorporated into that aspect of the on-the-spot investigation, or perhaps Lester simply carried medical evidence down to Dawson, and was held as a material witness in case it became necessary to prove the connection.

The trial took place in Dawson, but not until a year later.[11] O'Brien was sentenced to death on 22 June 1901 (the sentence was carried out at the Dawson Police Barracks on 23 August) and, on 31 July 1901, RRCI Regimental Order No. 176 reported the "No. 5068 Corporal E. Lincoln having returned from the Yukon is posted to No. 5 Company." It was thus his distinction to be the last man of the Yukon Field Force to leave the Territory.

* * * * * * * * * *

What happened to the men and women mentioned in Lester's pages? Well, Faith Fenton got married (on the first New Year's Day of the present century) to Dr. J.N.E. Brown, a mild-mannered medical man who was then working as secretary to the Yukon Commissioner and his Council, and who subsequently served as the Dawson district's Medical Officer of Health. In 1906 the

Browns returned to Toronto, where he opened a practice and she became a pillar of Toronto Society, the subject of romantic and wildly inaccurate stories of her Yukon days until her death in 1936[12]

The four VON nurses did sterling work in Dawson, and Dr. J.W. Good, the Medical Officer for Dawson in 1899, thought that:

> The only fault to be found with the present contingent is their small number; there is room here for a much larger body. If all patients could receive the careful nursing which is given by these devoted women, the mortality would be substantially decreased. The Order has, I believe, some opponents in the older Provinces — but the Victorian Order of Nurses will be warmly welcomed here.[13]

Lady Aberdeen must have been very happy.

In due course Margaret Payson took a position at the Dawson Post Office, married a wealthy miner, and "kept cats and dogs to her heart's content"; Amy Scott had to leave "owing to a serious operation", but subsequently served with the 10th Canadian Field Hospital in South Africa. Georgia Powell was also with the Field Hospital in South Africa and was awarded a Red Cross medal for her work there. She eventually married an NWMP sergeant. Rachel Hanna was for many years matron of St. Andrew's Hospital in Atlin, B.C.[14] and — at the age of 48! — was one of the one hundred nursing sisters who accompanied the Canadian Contingent overseas, in October 1914.

The Veterans

Since personnel records relating to the Canadian Militia prior to the First World War were destroyed during the 1930s, it is difficult to trace the subsequent careers of Lester's comrades — Platt, Spence, Sergeant Lapierre, McGowan, Kelly, and the rest. No doubt some served in South Africa and many more of the younger ones must have enlisted in the Canadian Expeditionary Force that went to Flanders fields in 1915. But, unless they distinguished themselves in some way, only chance can bridge the gap between their Yukon Field Force days and service on the South African veldt or the Western Front between 1914 and 1918. Three who did notably well were Sergeant William Rhoades, RCD, whose letter on the rigours of the Teslin trail provides a footnote for the diary entry of 23 July 1898, Corporal Michael Docherty, RCD, mentioned on 8 April 1899, and Bombardier William Kruger, who, together with a Private Fleming, was sent off to help in the construction of a NWMP post at Five Finger rapids on 4 October 1898. All three had been members of the advance guard on the trek north and among the fifty men sent on to Dawson shortly after the Force had arrived at Fort Selkirk. All were men of character who took real advantage of circumstance to better themselves. They saw service in South Africa and Flanders. Rhoades, who earned a rare peacetime commission from the ranks in his own exclusive regiment, and commanded the 5th Canadian Mounted Rifles during the First World War, earned a Distinguished Service Order and Bar, a Military Cross, and a *Croix de Guerre*, and was twice Mentioned in Despatches. Docherty commanded Lord Strathcona's Horse in 1917-18 and also won a DSO. Kruger won an MC and was also Mentioned in Despatches, eventually retiring as a lieutenant-colonel.[15]

Corporal J.W. Coupe, who first appears in the diary on 16 July, was another who later won a commission. He was a lieutenant-quartermaster while the RCR was garrisoning Bermuda in February 1915 and went with the battalion to France in November as its paymaster. Cpls. Blake-Forster (20 June 1898) and Moore (18 August 1898) and Ptes. Fleming and Graham (11 June 1898) all rose at least to the rank of quartermaster-sergeant and were awarded Long Service and Good Conduct Medals at various dates between 1911 and 1922. Blake-Forster and Sgt. Bingham (9 March 1899) each received a Meritorious Service Medal in 1918.[16]

As for the three men Lester mentions who died at Fort Selkirk, Corcoran (27 September 1898),Hansen (18 February 1899), and Walters (28 February 1899), they, together with Corporal M. Watson who died at Dawson in March 1900, and their commanding officer, Evans, are commemorated in the names of five minor peaks in the vicinity of Fort Selkirk. Jerry Corcoran may well be the first Canadian who died of drink to be immortalized for that very reason, but as the magazine *North* observed in reporting the event in 1972, "little is known about the four soldiers".

Field Force Officers

Among the officers, Colonel Evans distinguished himself again in South Africa, earning a a Companionship of the Bath and a commendation from General Hutton, who had also gone there, as "by far the best officer among the Mounted troops".[17] After the war he demonstrated social skills, as well as military ones, by marrying the daughter of the lieutenant-governor of Manitoba, Sir D.H. McMillan. In March 1907 he was promoted to the rank of full colonel and appointed District Officer Commanding, Military District No. 10, with its headquarters at Winnipeg. His future seemed assured when he suddenly fell victim to "heat prostration and overwork" and died in August 1908.[18]

Captain Charles St. Aubyn Pearse, RCD, went to South Africa with his regiment in February 1900, was wounded by Boer shrapnel, and died of pneumonia in a Pretoria hospital in November. Captain Edward Gardiner, RCD, also went to South Africa, but with the 2nd Canadian Mounted Rifles, a few weeks after his regiment had returned to Canada. He died in 1904.

Captain J.H.C. Ogilvie went to South Africa with the First Contingent, as adjutant of the Special Service battalion of the RCR. He distinguished himself at Paardeberg and Israel's Poorte, but when the battalion came home, Ogilvie stayed on, accepting an appointment in the South African Constabulary with the rank of major. He died of wounds received at Klipgat in December 1901.

Major David Douglas Young held various regimental and staff appointments until he retired in 1911. Surgeon-Major Gilbert Foster, and Captains Henry Burstall and Percy Thacker, all reached the rank of major-general in the First World War, and Henry Burstall (who had served with Ogilvie in South Africa) was knighted for his services. Foster died in 1940, Burstall and Thacker both lived until 1945. Lieutenant Louis Leduc served in South Africa and then rose to the rank of colonel in the CEF, retiring in 1924 and dying in France nine years later.[19]

Major Donald Cameron Forster Bliss's career followed a more irregular pattern, a spectacular example of character and circumstance, for better or worse. He was recalled from the Yukon under a cloud after a Mr. MacFarlane wrote to Evans, in early November 1899, lamenting that Bliss had failed to pay an outstanding bill of nearly $1,800. Bliss had bought certain goods from him that spring, resold them, and then neglected to pay off his supplier. There had been a number of earlier complaints, from the Hudson's Bay Company and the Canadian Bank of Commerce among others, concerning Bliss's cavalier handling of his financial affairs.

Bliss took the attitude that these were all private matters, entirely unconnected with his official duties or position, and therefore no concern of the Department's. Until the arrival of MacFarlane's denunciation, Colonel Evans seems to have accepted this view. After all, Bliss was a good officer, more than competent at his work, and a personal friend of long standing. There may have been social ties, too, between Evans' Ottawa relatives and the family of Bliss's wife, a daughter of Senator (and Privy Councillor) John Costigan, a former federal cabinet minister.

However, Evans was now about to relinquish command and could hardly leave this problem to be dealt with by his successor. He felt compelled to advise Ottawa that "Maj. Bliss's conduct with regard to money matters is now generally known in Dawson and throughout the Territory, and is doing grave injury to the good name of the Force under my command and the Militia of Canada", and recommended his recall.[20] On 1 January 1900 General Hutton wrote to the Deputy Minister of Militia and Defence agreeing that Bliss should be recalled and suggesting that he be placed on the Retired List. A minute by the Minister, Dr. Borden, approved of that solution, noting that there was no need to replace him now that the Force's strength had been reduced.[21]

Back in Ottawa, in semi-disgrace, Bliss set about rehabilitating himself. Evans, who had returned six weeks earlier, had gone off to South Africa, where he was to take command of the 2nd Battalion, Canadian Mounted Rifles (soon to be re-designated simply as the Canadian Mounted Rifles). Shortly after Evans took over his new command, however, Bliss was 'un-retired' and "attached to the 2nd Battalion, CMR, for duty with the machine-gun section, with the rank of lieutenant". He sailed to join Evans in mid-March 1900.

During the eight months that he was with the CMR, Bliss had no opportunity to distinguish himself. But after the CMR returned to Canada the guerrilla war in South Africa spluttered on and, in December 1901, Evans was tapped to command a second regiment of Canadian Mounted Rifles sent out to help the British mop up the last of the Boer commandos. There was tremendous competition among the officers of the Volunteer Militia for appointments in the latest contingent and Evans was unable to find a vacancy for his old friend. Nothing daunted, Bliss enlisted as a trooper.

Promptly promoted to sergeant, this time Bliss earned a Mention in Despatches from Lord Kitchener, and a Distinguished Conduct Medal (one of sixteen awarded to Canadians during the war), won back his commission in the field and returned to Canada a lieutenant and something of a hero. Ottawa decided that his rehabilitation was complete and he was given a majority in the newly created Ordnance Stores Corps of the Permanent Force. Posted to Quebec City as Superintendent of Stores, he was promoted to lieutenant-colonel in 1905 and subsequently transferred to Winnipeg, where — was it by chance?— Colonel T.D.B. Evans was in command. He retired in 1909, a year after Evans' death.

In May 1915, at the age of 54, he enlisted in the ranks once again, taking ten years off his age and giving his civilian occupation as "driver" in order to do so. He was assigned to the Canadian Veterinary Corps and posted to a remount depot in France, then served with the British artillery (who briefly commissioned him, but the arrangement was immediately cancelled) and ended the war as a staff sergeant-major with the Canadian Army Service Corps. He took his discharge in the United Kingdom and died at Glasgow in February 1931, surely one of the few men to have been commissioned three separate times by British monarchs.[22]

Edward Lester

As for Edward Lester, character and circumstance conspired against him. At first all went well. Back from the Yukon, he was posted to Quebec City, where a company of what was now the

Royal Canadian Regiment had been stationed since 1899. By June 1902 he was serving as hospital-sergeant (a warrant officer rank) at No. 4 Regimental Depot, Fredericton, but on the 4th of that month he was shown in orders as reverting to sergeant. Some time in the next ten months he was posted back to St. Johns, for on 18 April 1903 he was "reduced to the rank of Corporal by sentence of District Court Martial for the offence of Drunkenness on duty" there. An interesting aspect of his trial was his plea for mitigation of the inevitable sentence.

> Since my return from the Youkon [sic] I have had a good deal of family and private trouble and have been drinking perhaps more than I should do. I should like to draw the attention of the court to the fact that I have no Regimental entry [on my crime sheet] between 7 December 1895 and the summer of 1901, after my return from the Yukon.[23]

There are two points to be made about that statement: first, there is a clear implication that he had already been in disciplinary trouble at least once after his return from the Yukon; second, his reference to "family and private trouble", almost certainly concerned his association with Adelie Alicia Langille, 22 years his junior and the wife of an old Field Force associate and fellow sergeant, Robert Langille.[24] In January 1904 Adelie would give birth to a son that Lester acknowledged to be his,[25] confirmation of a relationship which had probably developed prior to his court martial and would last for the rest of their lives.

Langille, first mentioned in the diary on 2 June 1898 when the Field Force was kicking its heels at Glenora, and a corporal according to the entry of 10 March 1899 had left the Yukon with the group that went out with Major Young in September 1899. In 1902 he had gone to South Africa with the rank of squadron sergeant-major in the 4th Canadian Mounted Rifles, who arrived at the Cape within days of the signing of a peace treaty with the Boers and were shipped home again almost immediately. At that time Langille had been a single man but apparently sometime after his return in August 1902 he had married Adelie Paterson, who hailed from the Gaspé.

There was only one company of troops in the St. Johns garrison in 1903, eighty or ninety men all told, living in a highly cohesive environment within a small Quebec town. The Lester-Langille affair must have been widely known and the subject of general gossip. It seems unlikely that it met with much approval among the officers and senior NCOs, and once Lester had been reduced to

"All that is left of us, left of 200." Yukon Field Force veterans serving at Petawawa, Ont., militia camp, 1908. Lester is seated 2nd from right.

corporal his fate was probably sealed, since Robert Langille held the appointment of provost sergeant — a sort of combination policeman-gaoler to the unit! Making off with the provost sergeant's wife was a guaranteed way to demotion and the company paylist records summarily that Lester "Reverted to the ranks 9 July", presumably for a disciplinary offence which did not warrant a court martial. Then, in January 1904, came the birth of his son. When his current three-year engagement expired in March, he took his discharge and was released with the rank of private and a character assessed as only "Fair" after nine years' service.[26]

After his separation from the army Lester spent nearly three years in civilian life, a period about which nothing is known except that he and Adelie had another child. On 4 January 1907, at Toronto, he re-enlisted in the Royal Canadian Regiment, a step only possible because he was still technically a single man. He promptly remustered into the Army Medical Corps, which had been formed — as a result of the South African enlightenment — while he was out of the service. His past training and nursing experience should have served him well in his new branch, but again something went wrong. When his engagement expired in 1910 he re-enlisted in the Royal Canadian Dragoons; six months later he purchased his discharge and set himself up as a 'druggist' in Toronto.

On 25 April 1914 he married Adelie at Fordwich, Ontario, but we do not know whether any of their *six* children were at the wedding. On the marriage certificate they were identified as widower and widow respectively — the first Mrs. Lester had presumably been the mysterious 'M' of the diary — and Pension Commission files confirm that Adelie's spouse, Robert Langille, had, indeed, died, and that the Commissioners had seen the death certificate.[27]

Whether 'M' was really dead is a moot question not likely to be answered now. When Adelie applied for a widow's pension on the death of her second husband, twenty years later, there was no evidence of the demise of Lester's first wife, other than Adelie's recollection that Lester had once told her that the lady "had died in Australia, in about 1899". If that were really so, and Lester knew of it, it might have earned an entry in the diary. After all, on 7 February 1899 he had reported 'M' 's mother's death. In fact, a claim that 'M' had died in England could have been easily checked through the comprehensive and centralized records of Somerset House, in London. But Australia was another matter. A continent rather than a nation in 1899, it was then six separate colonies, each of them with an open frontier and its own inchoate record system, and checking out Lester's claim would have been extremely difficult and would probably have brought uncertain answers. Was

Lester's second marriage a bigamous one?

His business can hardly have been prospering. Otherwise, why would a 54-year-old man with a wife and growing family have thrown everything up to join the Canadian Expeditionary Force a year later? The same age as Donald Forster Bliss, he also falsified his age by ten years — but not his name this time — in order to get accepted into the 33rd Battalion, recruiting in London, Ontario, in July 1915. Shipped overseas as an acting corporal, Lester never got near a battlefield, however. He was soon suffering from chronic nephritis and spent most of his time in military hospitals in England until he was finally discharged in Toronto on 17 November 1917. His disability, attributed to service life, was assessed at 30% at that time.[28]

The Toronto directories for 1918 and 1919 again list him as a druggist, but by 1920 he is merely an 'agent'. His health had begun to deteriorate and in 1928 he was undergoing treatment for glaucoma and "cardio-renal" disease. By 1933 he was assessed as a "total disability" pensioner and shortly after one eye had to be surgically removed. He was in and out of hospital, and in 1935 his doctor was characterizing him as "a very difficult, old, blind man, cantankerous and unappreciative. He frequently falls but will not stay in the bed or chair where he is put". In November 1935 he broke his leg in one of those falls and four months later "he is confined to bed ... he is blind as well, and is mentally clouded". When he died, in the Christie Street Hospital on 23 May 1938, aged 77, it was noted that, for the past decade, "he has been for the most part, a bed patient and has been almost totally blind".[29]

Adelie, "mentally bright" to the end, died of cancer exactly two months later.

END NOTES

1. Evans to Chief Staff Officer, Ottawa, 23 November 1899, in PAC, RG 9, II, Vol. 312. This was Evans' final report.
2. Ogilvie to Sifton, 12 November 1898, in Sifton Papers, PAC, MG 27, II, D 15, Vol. 295.
3. GOC Militia to Minister of Militia and Defence, 29 May 1899, in PAC, RG 9, II, B 1, Vol. 284, f. 77933.
4. US State Department to Minister of Militia and Defence, 12 August 1899, in *ibid.*
5. Chief Staff Officer, Ottawa, to OC, Yukon Force, 28 July 1899, in *ibid.*

6. R.C. Fetherstonhaugh, The Royal Canadian Regiment 1883-1933, (Montreal, 1936), p. 77.
7. Sworn declaration by L.A. Pare, dated 15 February 1900, in PAC, RG 18, Vol. 3413, file 3744, and Comptroller, NWMP, to Secretary, Dept. of Militia and Defence, 6 May 1901, in PAC, RG 9, II, B 1, Vol. 326.
8. R.C. Fetherstonhaugh, loc. cit., p. 78.
9. OC, NWMP, Yukon Territory, to Deputy Adjutant-General, Ottawa, 20 November 1900, in PAC, RG 9, II, Vol. 327, ff. 92649.
10. A transcript of the trial is in PAC, RG 13, C 1, Vol. 1440.
11. M.J. Malcolm, Murder In The Yukon: The Case Against George O'Brien (Saskatoon, Sask., 1982) has a full account.
12. Obituary, Toronto Mail and Empire, 11 January 1936.
13. J.M. Gibbon, The Victorian Order of Nurses for Canada 50th Anniversary 1897-1947 (Ottawa, 1947), p. 34.
14. "Rachel Hanna's Diary", in Bracebridge Herald-Gazette, 11 April 1974; J.M. Gibbon, loc. cit. pp. 34 -5.
15. Personnel records, Public Archives Record Centre (PARC); Militia Lists.
16. R.C. Fetherstonhaugh, loc. cit., pp. 188, passim.
17. Hutton to Minto, 30 October 1900, in Minto Papers, PAC, MG 27, II, B2, Vol. 16.
18. Obituary, Manitoba Free Press, 24 August 1908.
19. Jackson Lists, D. Hist, and personnel records, PARC.
20. Evans to Chief Staff Officer, Ottawa, 23 November 1899, loc. cit.
21. GOC Militia to Deputy Minister, 1 January 1900, in PAC, RG 9, II, B 1, Vol. 312; Militia Order No. 3, 11 January 1900.
22. Militia Order No. 69 of 24 March 1900; London Gazette, 29 July, 31 October, 1902; and 24 February 1903. Personnel records, RG 38, 1 A, Vol. 9 and PARC.
23. RCR Regimental Orders, Nos. 208 of 9 June 1902, 235 of 22 April 1903 and 403 of 19 July 1907, in RCR Archives, Wolseley Barracks, London, Ontario; King's Regulations and Orders for the Canadian Militia,1906; Lester to Pension Commissioners, 28 September 1920, in PAC Reference file 1536; DVA microfilm reel VF-31; CEF Personnel file, PARC, and PAC, RG9, II, B 1, Vol. 467, No. 1672/03.
24. RCR Paylist, May 1903, in PAC, RG 9, II, F8, Vol. 35.
25. DVA microfilm reel VF-31, DVA Ottawa.
26. Register of Enlistments, RCR Archives, loc. cit.
27. DVA microfilm reel VF-31
28. CEP Personnel record, PARC.
29. DVA microfilm reel VF-31.

Illustration Credits

All illustrations are from the Public Archives of Canada with the following exceptions.

Glenbow Museum pages 76,80,160,187
Provincial Archives of British Columbia page 62
The Royal Canadian Dragoons Archives page 27
The Royal Canadian Regiment Archives page 173

.

www.ingramcontent.com/pod-product-compliance
Lightning Source LLC
Chambersburg PA
CBHW060745100426
42813CB00032B/3406/J